INFINITE PURPOSE

CARE INSTRUCTIONS FOR YOUR TRUE CALLING

Liv Lane & Lori Portka

ISBN 13: 978-1-63489-004-5

Library of Congress Catalog Number: 2015946947

Printed in Canada

First Printing: 2015

19 18 17 16 15   5 4 3 2 1

Cover and interior design by Emily Shaffer Rodvold at Lift Creative.
Author photos by Tera Girardin of Tera Photography.

Wise Ink Creative Publishing

837 Glenwood Avenue

Minneapolis, MN 55405

wiseinkpub.com

To order, visit itascabooks.com or call 1-800-901-3480.

Reseller discounts available.

Table of Contents

DEDICATIONS

FROM LIV

To my beautiful boys, Ryder and Truman, for all you teach me.
To my loving husband, Brad, for stepping into the wild unknown with me.
And to my dear mom for always believing in me.

FROM LORI

To my husband, Jay, for fiercely believing in our big vision
for this book even when I wavered. Thank you for being my
sounding board and my sweetheart. I adore you.

GRAT

WE ARE TRULY AWESTRUCK BY the incredible support we've received from so many generous and gifted souls to birth this book into the world.

It all started with more than 250 open-minded mavericks who signed up for the original *Infinite Purpose* online course in 2014. Witnessing their growth and excitement deeply inspired us, and their continued support has bowled us over. Special thanks to the sixteen brave hearts who shared their powerful, inspiring stories for this book.

Every page was crafted with ten-der loving care, thanks to a dedicated and gifted team of creatives. We loved working with Wise Ink Creative Publishing and are especially grateful for cofounder Amy Quale's vision, guidance, and passion throughout. Editor Alison Watts and proofreader Darlinda Alexander worked their magic with our words, and designer Emily Shaffer Rodvold brought our visions of the book to life.

Our circle of miracle workers extends beyond the publication process. We've been so blessed to collaborate with generous and gifted creatives

TUDE

who have rallied around this project, including Tera Girardin of Tera Photography, Kristi Roehm of 8 DEGREES, Lisa Dubbels of Catalyst Publicity, Laurel Bleadon-Maffei, and Lynn O'Brien.

But this book might not even exist without the tidal wave of support we received during our crowdfunding campaign. We're so grateful to everyone who contributed and preordered, ensuring we could afford the costs of production and our first printing without comprising the quality of the book. Thank you!

There are so many friends, relatives, mentors, and supporters who have encouraged us along the way—far too many to list! But we cannot send this book into the world without remembering our dads, Peter Benson and Joseph Portka, who always encouraged us to follow our hearts. We know they've been by our sides throughout this project, sending us signs from beyond and wrapping us in love.

Finally, we are profoundly grateful to Spirit for entrusting us with these sacred teachings and, in doing so, nudging us deeper into our own true callings.

WELCOME TO YOUR INFINITE PURPOSE

THERE'S A GOOD REASON YOU'RE HOLDING THIS TREASURE OF A BOOK. It was carefully, lovingly, and purposefully made for *you*. No matter how this book made its way into your hands, the teachings within are divinely designed to work their way into your heart and enrich your life in miraculous ways. You think you found this book, but the truth is, it found you. Whether whispering to the stars above or shaking your fists at goals unmet, you have let the universe know that you're ready for something more. You're craving clear direction, dreaming of greater abundance, longing for lasting fulfillment, and eager to enhance what makes your life—and the work you're here to do—so meaningful.

WE KNOW BECAUSE WE'VE BEEN THERE. AND BECAUSE WE'VE BEEN ASKED TO HELP.

We feel like the luckiest friends on the planet, thrust into the heart-thumping, soul-stirring collaboration you now hold in your hands. I'm Liv, your narrator for this grand adventure, and Lori's here too, paintbrushes in hand. This book contains teachings gifted to us by Spirit (we may never get over the amazingness of this!), offered with the understanding we'd bring them to *life*—literally and figuratively. We've put our hearts and souls into doing just that, creating a guidebook rich with personal stories, visual inspiration, and sacred space for reflection to augment Spirit's powerful eight-step path to purpose.

So, imagine us watching you now with great anticipation, eyes wide with hope as you unwrap this gift. We can't wait to see how you receive it. We so hope you love it, use it, trust it, learn from it, scribble in it, keep returning to it, and see your bright future in it.

Let's get started. . . .

FINDING LIGHT IN THE DARK

The content and publication of this book evolved at light speed, but we now see the foundation for it was laid years ago. It all began five weeks into 2003 with both of us in bed, curled up in the fetal position, many miles apart, and unaware the other existed. Lori and I were each struggling for different reasons. We barely had the strength to make it through each winter day, much less see that we were being guided to a great awakening and, with divine timing, to each other.

At age twenty-eight, I was living the American dream. I was running a media subsidiary I'd started for a major corporation, living in a South Minneapolis bungalow with my husband Brad, and eagerly awaiting the arrival of our first baby. Life was really good—until I went into labor. A bevy of complications and miscommunications led to a traumatic birth experience for me and our baby boy, Ryder George, who arrived black and blue and barely breathing. Though Ryder made an amazing recovery in the NICU, I didn't fare as well. At home, I barely slept or ate, and whenever the baby cried, it sent ripples of terror through my body. I remember collapsing into bed one afternoon, wincing at the way our normally soft comforter felt like needles on my skin, ashamed for not feeling happy after taking home a miraculously *healthy* baby, and wanting to scream with rage over my new life.

Little did I know that exactly 1,122 miles away, thirty-three-year-old Lori was going through the very same thing, curled up in bed and devastated over a life change *she* didn't want. From the outside looking in, Lori had been living the dream, too. She and her husband had just bought a house in upstate New York where they'd been offered teaching jobs in the same school district. Lori stayed behind in Maryland to sell their house and complete her Master's degree in counseling, excited for their future in New York. But while they were apart, Lori's husband began to drink daily, and there were plenty of indications he was cheating on her, too. Lori was committed to their marriage and longed for a fresh start, but several months after she joined him in New York, her husband announced he wanted a divorce. There were no discussions to be had, no negotiations to be made, and no attempts at reconciliation. He wanted out and Lori's world caved in.

Too humiliated and hurt to see him every day at work, Lori left town with $250 in coins she'd found at their house, grateful to have just enough for gas and to pay the deposit on a one-bedroom apartment. She found a low-paying job conducting early interventions for children with special needs, and for the next year, she would crumple into bed after work each day and cry. Worried she was spiraling down into the chronic depression that her mom had long struggled with, Lori decided some serious self-care was in order, from regularly attending Al-Anon meetings (for loved ones of those struggling with addiction) to reading *The Artist's Way* by Julia Cameron. Lori had loved drawing as a girl but never dared to create anything while married to an art teacher, worried that her work wouldn't measure up. Tired of sleeping away her afternoons, she started to paint. First, she painted a plain kitchen stool, then pictures of her friends' dogs, and, eventually, images of happy women. For the first time in a long time, Lori felt alive.

Meanwhile, with prompting from my worried family, I began extensive treatment for postpartum depression (PPD) and post-traumatic stress disorder (PTSD), slowly moving out of the shadows and back into my life. One day in 2006, while walking through our family room, I was stopped in my tracks by an unfamiliar voice. That's right—*a voice*. In fact, it sounded like a choir of many speaking in perfect harmony—deep and authoritative, but also kind and comforting—and it said this: "Photograph and write about something beautiful every day for a year." The directions were so specific, and seemed so life-affirming, that I couldn't ignore the message. Days later, I started a blog, posting daily photos and reflections of beauty in my midst, amazed by the joy that came from it and awed by the wide response to it. For the first time in a long time, I felt alive, too.

Those flickers of hope for Lori and me—the chance to create something good in our corners of the world—saved us from ourselves. Over the next few years, our lives slowly transformed as we immersed ourselves in our passions, leaving our jobs to build our businesses, and allowing our hearts to open again. Lori remarried after meeting the love her life, Jay, at an Al-Anon meeting in 2005. And I gained enough courage to have another baby, bringing bright-light Truman into the world in 2008. Life was good again, which felt like a miracle to both of us. But we had no idea how much better it could get.

THE GREAT BEYOND

When Lori and I first met at a small art retreat in 2010, it felt like a reunion, as if we'd

known each other forever. Talking deep into the night about everything under the sun, I felt instantly safe with her. Safe enough, in fact, to reveal what only a handful of confidants knew. When I was growing up, I told Lori, I regularly saw and heard angels and spirits—in the yard, in my bedroom, and even at school. Once I realized other kids didn't see the same things, I grew self-conscious. I did my best to avoid and bury those abilities through my twenties, worried people would call me crazy if they knew. But with the inner work I'd done to heal my mental health, my intuitive gifts had come roaring back in, harder than ever to hide.

Lori was not spooked by my stories of connecting with the Other Side, but fascinated and, to my surprise, comforted. "Ever since my dad died when I was fifteen, I have felt him around me, like his spirit was still living," she told me, her eyes welling with tears. "But my family didn't believe in God or an afterlife or angels. Hearing your experiences gives me more faith in mine."

Over the next couple of years, Lori and I both opened our hearts wider to the presence and power of unseen forces at work, growing less scared of sounding crazy and more concerned with not following our callings. Lori began quietly requesting the angels' guidance before beginning a painting and marveled at the ways her business took flight. I started doing private readings for friends, and eventually for perfect strangers, sharing guidance for them from the Other Side.

Sometimes the angels and spirits flash images for me to describe to my clients. Other times they speak in full sentences, and it feels as though the words—and the emotion behind them—are downloaded to me, fed to me to say aloud. It's a little like having a song stuck in your head. You can practically hear it playing inside of you, and then you find yourself humming it out loud.

One morning in 2013, I was startled by a voice outside myself. It was the same crystal clear voice that had urged me to find beauty in my midst seven years before. I quickly scribbled down the words I heard: this voice belonged to Spirit, a circle of ascended wise ones in the Great Beyond. They were prepared to assist with my readings, they said, *and* provide divinely inspired direction for our larger work together. I had no idea what they meant by that but felt instantly humbled and awestruck by their invitation.

From that point on, Spirit showed up to help whenever I called upon them, from providing detailed guidance during private readings to helping me craft curriculum for group programs. That is, until one autumn day when they turned the tables by calling on *me*—and pulling in Lori, too. In the blink of an eye and a breathtaking merging of our paths, *Infinite Purpose* was born.

A SPIRITED COLLABORATION

In the fall of 2014, I kept seeing images of Lori's paintings flash before my eyes and suspected it meant some sort of collaboration was in our future. But I couldn't bear to bother Lori; she was immersed in a big project for a major publisher, producing dozens of paintings on a tight deadline. Whatever we were meant to work on could wait, I figured.

But the universe has its own timetable. One afternoon, Lori texted me with tough news: the publisher had just rejected eight of her paintings and she was devastated, having put so much time and energy into them. As soon as I read her text, it felt as though a lightning bolt jolted through my body. As I leaned against the kitchen counter for support, I heard Spirit's voice vibrating around and through me. "Those paintings are meant for *you*," they said. "To say they were *rejected* is a misnomer, for they were explicitly chosen for a divinely guided collaboration called *Infinite Purpose*."

"What!? When!? How!?" I begged for more details, but they said nothing more.

As soon as I regained my composure, I told Lori, "I don't know what is happening, but when Spirit stops me in my tracks with instructions, I know something big is in the works." Together, we decided not to panic and, instead, to trust that God had a plan, Spirit had the details, and it would all unfold perfectly.

Spirit returned days later with more details, giving us one month to build and gather participants for an online program focused on "living with enhanced purpose, set to the vibration of abundance." Spirit assured us that no fancy marketing was necessary to attract the "right" people to these teachings. Rather, they'd see themselves reflected in the following description and sense it was meant for them:

"We seek those in flow, aligned with their calling. And those seeking flow, feeling pulled into greater purpose," Spirit said. "Emerging leaders, creative visionaries, gifted messengers, and impassioned change agents. We shall serve as an ascended midwife, actively aiding the birth of their visions and revealing the divine care instructions for purpose personified."

The messages, Spirit said, would be "momentum-building missives, ensuring abundant growth and growing abundance in their evolving vocations."

Each week for eight weeks, Spirit instructed, I would need to transcribe their in-depth teachings word-for-word. We would see elements of their messages already painted into being in Lori's artwork, Spirit said, and she'd be asked to add some of their words to her creations. Honestly, it was hard for us to wrap our minds around these directions. I was accustomed to relaying, in my own words, Spirit's insights for clients. But receiving and transcribing page after page of messaging—the kind capable of altering people's livelihoods—would require a new level of focus and trust. And even though Lori's creative ritual included asking the angels for help with her art, she was astonished to hear that Spirit had swooped in to inspire the subject matter of those eight paintings, ensuring each had just enough space to add their words of wisdom.

With knees knocking, we posted Spirit's description of the program online. What happened next blew us away. In a matter of days, over 250 people around the world registered for *Infinite Purpose*. Once the program began, we were amazed by what transpired. Over and over, we witnessed the wisdom of Spirit's teachings impact participants' lives in miraculous ways, from jaw-dropping opportunities to life-changing revelations. And we both experienced so much magic in our own lives, too! By the time the program was over, our hearts were full with wonder and awe, but our heads were spinning.

Spirit let us rest for a couple of weeks, allowing us to ease back into our routines at home and work. And then, images began to flash before me again—this time, of a book. I let Lori know via text, and she replied right away. "I have felt like Spirit wanted me to start making art for something," she wrote. "Stories keep flying into my head, and little signs and messages keep appearing. It's like, this time I can *feel* them working with me—ALL THE TIME."

Within a couple of days, Spirit brought me new information. The online dissemination of their teachings had only been the beginning of our collaboration, they said. Lori and I had needed to personally witness and experience the impact of *Infinite Purpose* in order to willingly and joyfully work to expand its reach. But this time, they said, we would include *our* story.

It was Spirit who revealed to us the synergy of our journeys. Over the years, we'd briefly spoken of challenges we'd overcome, but we spent most of our time talking about current events and future dreams. So when Spirit instructed us to share with each other what our lives were like in early 2003, we were absolutely stunned. It brought us to tears, knowing we were both curled up in despair at the very same time. The life events that felt like torture, Spirit pointed out, invited us to pave new paths and heal our hearts through creativity, connection, and the cultivation of joy, which, quite intentionally, led us to each other and into the light of infinite purpose.

"Spirit has had a hand in our friendship all along," Lori said breathlessly. That realization made it easy to say yes to their newest request—writing this book.

As soon as we agreed to move forward, Spirit swiftly delivered the perfect partners and circumstances to birth this book into being, assuring us that it would organically work its way into the lives of dear hearts like *you*—on purpose. It was crafted with so much love and light, and we're eager to help you leverage it in ways that will catapult you toward the brave and blissful work you're here to do.

HOW THIS BOOK WORKS

You are about to embark on a remarkable journey through Spirit's eight-step path to purpose. Their teachings are featured in eight separate sections meant to be read and experienced *in order* for the greatest impact. Spirit says the energetic vibration of each step is calibrated to flow into the next, activating the deliberate expansion of your path each time you advance. As you dedicate yourself fully to this divinely designed process, embracing the guided reflections and inspired actions these teachings call for, you allow shifts to take place in your head *and* heart that open the floodgates to goodness. Ideas, opportunities, connections, revelations, invitations, and inspirations will appear out of the blue when you're ready for them.

Lori and I begin each section with our own behind-the-scenes story or *holy wow* moment to prepare you for the teaching you're about to digest. This is really important to us, and we hope it's helpful to you. Although we've been gifted with these extraordinary messages, we're still just regular women—long distance friends with bills to pay, families to tend to, and kitchen counters to clean—doing our best to lead soulful, purposeful, and joyful lives. We figure maybe that's why Spirit chose us to bring their teachings down to earth, revealing what's possible when people like us—and like you—step into the light of their own purpose. Early on in Spirit's teachings, they used the term "magic makers" to refer to those drawn to these teachings, showing up to make magic. We fell in love with that description, so you might notice we use it often!

Following our short story at the start of each section, turn the page to find a gorgeous full-page painting by Lori with the theme of Spirit's next step written on it. Though I'd briefly seen some of the paintings via text weeks before, I couldn't recall any specifics about them. So, back when I was first transcribing the teachings for *Infinite Purpose*, Spirit would repeatedly flash an image for me until I'd seen just enough detail—like a house or a bike—to accurately describe it to Lori. Spirit would then give me one sentence meant to be handwritten on the painting as well as incorporated into their next teaching. Lori and I were repeatedly wowed by the ways in which the art and words aligned so beautifully.

On the page opposite each painting, the next step—or teaching—begins beneath the words "Message from Spirit." Some people say I channeled these messages, but I felt more like a courtroom stenographer, typing the words exactly as I heard them. No one took over my body, and I was mildly aware of everyday distractions, from the dog barking to my kids playing down the hall, but I kept typing with my eyes

closed to help me focus on Spirit's voice. Once each message was complete, which often took many hours, Lori and I were stunned by what had come through. For one thing, the writing was so distinctly different from my own voice—so elegant, eloquent, and clever that I sometimes had to look up a word to see what it meant! There is deep intention behind every word Spirit uses and *how* they use it. For instance, they would frequently request that I capitalize certain words like Goodness or All of Creation to signify that they were speaking of a boundless universe and omnipresent life force too holy to define with just one word and too multifaceted for us to fully comprehend.

At first, we were also surprised to find that Spirit had assigned homework for each lesson. But each assignment is so powerful that the homework has become one of our favorite aspects of their teachings. We've found that those who take the time to thoughtfully approach Spirit's prompts often experience major shifts in mindset and an acceleration in goal manifestation. To make this easier for you, we've included pages at the end of each message outlining Spirit's latest assignment. Think of these pages as a sacred space to hold what excites you, scares you, moves you, and reconnects you to your soul's purpose. Overflowing with insights? There are blank pages at the back of this book for additional reflections. And if you'd like to revisit an assignment, you can print out extra worksheets from our website. Gain exclusive access at **yourinfinitepurpose.com/resources** and input the password MAGICMAKERS.

Finally, we know you want to hear how this process has impacted others. Each section ends with stories of brave hearts who were kind enough to share how a particular step—or the overall program—moved like wildfire through their lives to ignite their passions, open new doors, reveal new paths, create new connections, seize joy, and do what once seemed impossible. We're so thrilled to share their stories and can't wait to hear *yours*.

We think it's important to share that while we were developing this book,

Spirit requested that small but important changes be made to their original texts. They called it a "vibrational attunement," ensuring that their teachings continue to resonate in this format. Every word on the page holds energy, Spirit says, so that "a galaxy of possibility exists in every sentence."

Lori and I are particularly awed by this: Spirit insists that this book was custom made for *you*. The teachings, they say, are intricately designed to uniquely impact each individual reader, with intermittent "pulse points" at which you may feel your heartbeat quicken as you read through statements that are energetically and intentionally aligned with who you are and what you need in that precise moment. So if it feels like a particular sentence was written for you, *it was*. No two people will experience *Infinite Purpose* in the exact same way, Spirit says—not in studying it *or* in living it.

As you move through the pages of this book and feel the vibration of these divine teachings lift you up and onto your enlightened path to deeper purpose, know that Spirit is supporting you at every step and that Lori and I are here, too, cheering wildly from the bleachers. Welcome to the team, magic maker.

HOW TO GET WHERE YOU'RE GOING

IF YOU'RE FEELING A TAD NERVOUS AS YOU DIVE INTO THIS BOOK, WE totally understand—and we think it's a good sign. Many performers say having nerves before hitting the stage indicates they still care about their craft and their audience. If they're not nervous, they're not fully invested in doing or being their best. Superstars know how to push through the fear, using that energy to fuel their performance rather than weaken it. The same applies here, don't you think? It would be odd not to feel some fear as you explore your calling and shine your light.

When Spirit first delivered their instructions for *Infinite Purpose*, revealing our roles as messengers of these teachings, Lori and I were awestruck, elated, and scared to pieces. Were we crazy to attach our names to content we'd never read? Would we come off as insane or pretentious or misguided? Was it irresponsible to set aside our workloads and devote so much energy to a project we knew next to nothing about?

Every time we'd spin our wheels, obsessing about what might go wrong, we'd always wind up here: we couldn't say no to something that felt so meaningful, so inspired, and so deeply needed. So we said yes—and it changed our lives *for good*.

Once we traded in fear for faith, we got so many signs that we were on the right path. For instance, when Spirit provided the exact date we were supposed to launch the original online program, we were shocked: we'd already planned to be together in New York City on that day, enjoying a girls' weekend that my husband had planned months before as a fortieth birthday present. Every stroke of synchronicity served as a reminder that we were part of something so much bigger than ourselves—something not to be afraid of, but to be in awe of.

Step One of *Infinite Purpose* invites you into a brand new world, with Spirit lovingly leading the way. So, tell your fear to take a hike. You're here because you're ready.

Choose to move off the beaten path and into the wild unknown

MESSAGE FROM SPIRIT

AND SO WE BEGIN. WE COMMEND YOU FOR ANSWERING THE CALL, FOR allowing yourself to be pulled into the unknown and trusting it will lead you Home. Indeed, it will. We will help.

We are a conglomerate of celestial guides—spiritual beings without form. We have walked in your shoes and down your roads before and know firsthand the weight of the world you live in. For centuries, we remained deeply connected and committed to our souls' missions, to God's vision for our lives there and elsewhere, because we could *feel* the blessing of being chosen, of being silently ordained as messengers and meaning-makers. We now do our work from beyond the physical realm.

We have been given the clear vision of Creation, of All That Is Good, for each and every one of you, granted access to your divinely inspired path and the possibilities it holds so that we might impart wisdom that both eases and accelerates your journey to purpose. Each of you has been called to these teachings because you have been chosen, explicitly, to carry out missions of light during your time on Earth.

You have felt this, yes? Even if ever so fleeting, you have had notions of being needed, feeling blessed with something you could not quite put your finger on, seeing what others could not or would not see, feeling and absorbing the energy of this time and place, and sometimes feeling alone in your hopefulness while the masses drunkenly drown in their misery. *You* are also part of a conglomerate of spiritual beings; specifically, a growing population of earthbound souls ready to realize their full potential, individually and collectively.

When we speak of potential, we are solely focused on all that matters: the creation, cultivation, and expansion of Perfect Love and the light that emanates from it. It is why you are here.

Behold the first painting by Lori, on page 16, which beautifully illustrates the way we see each of you beginning this journey. We see a clear path where you may not yet. We see you moving forward, led by your own gorgeous gifts—like the flowers in that basket leading this girl Home. They delight her, and they will delight others. She cannot wait to share them! To hide a gift from others because it may be too precious, too lovely, or too unique defeats the purpose of the gift. And so, the bicyclist will work her way to where she belongs, then carefully gather each blossom from her basket and carry them all together in a one-of-a-kind cornucopia of color and depth. Everyone who sees her will remark and ask questions about her beautiful bouquet. The story she tells about these flowers, of where she found them or how she grew them, will captivate each person, plant a seed in their own hearts, and pique their curiosity about what might grow and flourish if they, too, choose to move off the beaten path and into the wild unknown. For that is where the depth of your purpose is found.

Many of you have taken the first steps to remove yourself from the so-called rat race but are still running parallel to that well-worn road. Look at the painting again. She is so close to the edge, hugging the line between thinking and being. As is the case with *you*, beloved.

By moving off to the side, you hope to escape the congestion and potholes and happily pedal past the vehicles that are slowing to a crawl. There is a great rush that comes with this—a sense of victory as you breeze past those mighty machines that are stuck and stressing, honking and heaving. Still, you must be careful. You remain focused on the road, the vehicles beside you, and the traffic up ahead. If anyone swerves, opens their door, or picks up speed, you know it could alter your course, even throw you off and send you tumbling. Here is the truth: this hyper-focused exercise, fastidiously watching your fellow road warriors as you hug the curb, is more exhausting than you realize. You wind up spinning your wheels time and time again.

We ask today, beloved, that you begin to recognize how much time and energy you spend watching that road and its travelers, in tune with their expectations, gut-punched by their sideways glances, and playing tug-of-war with your ego on the sidelines. You may have moved out of the flow of traffic, out of step with convention, but it is still top of mind, isn't it? You still think about what others think, and then feel the wheels beneath you start to wobble. You pull over to adjust, to feel your feet on solid ground, before placing them back upon the pedals and hoisting yourself up. It takes effort to go from standing still to flying forward, but you get there (yet again), still hugging the side of the road, cautiously optimistic that you can get where you are going this time.

There is another way. It is our desire to guide you away from the main road, far from this mass-transit mindset and into the great unknown where you can pave your own path, undistracted and undeterred by what "everyone" says or does or thinks, and build momentum for your missions of the heart (even if you don't know what they are yet).

Perhaps it feels daring to go where there is no path before you, but look at what else is offered here. You will find fertile ground for growing and blooming while the well-beaten path remains barren. You have no choice but to rely on your inner guidance as your navigator. You will lead yourself to buried treasure, discover magic underfoot, and meet fellow travelers just as beautifully lost *and* found as you. Conventional wisdom will stay the course, coughing up exhaust as it barrels down the road you left behind, skidding back and forth from right to wrong, right to wrong. Once you detach from it, you see the insanity of it.

For travelers in the wild unknown, there is no speed limit to hold you back, no painted lines to cage you in, and no traffic stops to disrupt your momentum. Know that this may cause natural but unintended friction with comrades who have chosen to hang back, to stick to the roads most traveled, for your success stories will no longer match theirs. Your full-throttle life may look unwieldy and unstable to them. They will wonder how on earth you found your way without a map.

Let today be the day you join the wildflowers grown from the sacred, scattered seeds of divine possibility and infinite purpose. You see the vibrant blooms gathered in your basket, painted into being by Lori, plucked from the earth to provide fresh inspiration for your day? You'll no longer need to gather only as much as you can carry, for in the wild unknown, all that blooms is ever abundant. You shall be surrounded by All You Need and All That Inspires.

We ask you, as we begin this sacred journey with you, to call upon time-honored trailblazers. Please spend time with three who have inspired you, shaped you, and awed you. Read their stories, listen to their voices, and retrace their steps into the wild unknown. How did they get there? How did they stay there? How did they know where to go, what to do, and how to expand the light of their compassionate hearts and inventive minds? Let them be your teachers; let this be your homework. Study the wise ones, the wild ones.

You have been called to these teachings, beloved, to become courageously and joyfully immersed in purpose. The investments of time and energy which make *your* heart content will simultaneously guide the lost, awaken the sleeping, soften the hardened, heal the ailing, inspire the road-weary, color the sky, or reveal the truth.

You may feel stymied by setbacks. You might feel stuck at a crossroads. Perhaps you feel exhilarated and exhausted by the shifts of transition. Maybe you sense something new blooming in the shadow of heartbreak. As you move through each page of these transcendent teachings, know that you are being lovingly guided to create a new field, to establish a new way of being, and to experience and cultivate evolutionary, revolutionary bliss guided by, gifted with, and growing in the light.

So come now, beloved. It is time to leave behind the perceptions and prescriptions that ultimately hold you back—recipes for success, your stories of *not enough*, and fears you hold close so that no one else sees. We have been waiting for you. We rejoice in this moment, which marks the beginning of new things, of renewed things, of revered things. You are right where you belong.

REFLECTION ONE
Follow Your Trailblazers

IN STEP ONE, SPIRIT ASKS US TO DRAW INSPIRATION AND INSIGHTS FROM TIME-HONORED TRAILBLAZERS. USE THIS REFLECTION PAGE TO CHOOSE THREE PEOPLE (LEADERS, INNOVATORS, CHANGE-MAKERS, EARTH ANGELS) WHO HAVE "INSPIRED YOU, SHAPED YOU, AND AWED YOU." DIG DEEPER INTO THEIR BRAVE STORIES VIA BOOKS, ARTICLES, PODCASTS, MEDIA APPEARANCES, BLOGS, FAMILY STORIES, AND PERSONAL MEMORIES.

WHAT TO DO: Below, list each of your three chosen trailblazers and note what you find particularly fascinating and inspiring about the ways in which they stepped into the wild unknown. What motivated them to move off the beaten path? What choices did they make, what challenges did they overcome, what kept them inspired, and how did they add light to the world?

TRAILBLAZER ONE: ....
WHAT INSPIRES ME ABOUT HIS/HER JOURNEY:

....
....
....
....
....
....

TRAILBLAZER TWO: ....
WHAT INSPIRES ME ABOUT HIS/HER JOURNEY:

....

....

....

....

....

TRAILBLAZER THREE: ....
WHAT INSPIRES ME ABOUT HIS/HER JOURNEY:

....

....

....

....

....

Get Inspired! Examples of much-beloved trailblazers:

ELEANOR ROOSEVELT • OPRAH WINFREY
FRED ROGERS • DR. MARTIN LUTHER KING JR.
CHERYL STRAYED • MAHATMA GANDHI
PEMA CHODRON • DR. CHRISTIANE NORTHRUP
ELISABETH KÜBLER-ROSS • THICH NHAT HANH
MAYA ANGELOU • JOHN LENNON

INSPIRING STORIES OF INFINITE PURPOSE

A MINDFUL CAREER CHANGE

As soon as Sarah Rudell Beach saw Spirit's words on Lori's first painting—*choose to move off the beaten path and into the wild unknown*—she freaked out. "Those words were so scary because I *loved* the beaten path," Sarah told us. "I guess I'd hoped Spirit would tell me to play it safe!"

Sarah had spent seventeen years as a high school history teacher, a stable job she loved. But she couldn't shake the idea of pursuing one of her passions full time—writing and speaking about mindfulness for youth (and the grownups who parent and teach them).

The lack of a steady paycheck terrified her, but Sarah decided to push through the fear, focusing instead on growing something beautiful and sharing it with others—just like the woman in Lori's painting. As she moved through the steps of *Infinite Purpose*, opportunities for speaking and consulting serendipitously appeared. Within a couple of months, Sarah's school district had granted her a three- to five-year leave of absence, and she launched her new company, brilliantmindfulness.com.

"I'm following my bliss, stepping off the beaten path, with the gorgeous safety net of a career I still love if my path leads back to the classroom," Sarah said. "This is the absolute right step for me to pursue my deepest calling!"

CALLED TO AFRICA

For more than two decades, Jennifer Keenan has worked in a field she adores, developing special education curriculum and helping children with special needs through animal-assisted therapy. "There is no greater feeling than witnessing a child exceed expectations," she said. "Especially when they are doubted by many."

As soon as she read the first *Infinite Purpose* message, she was moved to write down the following vision for her life: "I will travel the world one day to work with children with special needs, and I really feel a pull towards Africa." When it came to naming trailblazers who inspired her, Jennifer decided to pray, asking that she be guided to someone doing the kind of work she had just visualized for herself.

A quick online search led Jennifer to a tribute for an African woman who had dedicated her life to caring for orphans with special needs. Through that post, she discovered a young American woman named Emma who was committed to following in that woman's footsteps by opening a special needs center in Uganda. Jennifer followed her instincts and sent Emma an email, asking how she could help. The response Jennifer received blew her away. Emma wrote that just two days before, she and a friend had asked God to send them someone to help establish their center.

Jennifer and her teenage daughter, Alana, who shares her mom's passion for helping children with special needs, launched a successful crowdfunding campaign, making it possible for them to travel to Kampala, Uganda—just six months after Jennifer wrote down her vision—with an abundance of materials and expertise to help the center there launch a comprehensive education program.

"Together, we are stepping off the beaten path and it's scary, but so worth it," Jennifer said before the trip. "We know we have an entire team working with us in spirit, and if we need help, all we have to do is ask."

STEP TWO

THE TRUTH ABOUT DREAMS

HAVE YOU EVER THOUGHT AN UNEXPECTED CHALLENGE WAS REALLY God working undercover to redirect you to something better? That's what happened when my travel plans tanked following a wonderful weekend in New York launching *Infinite Purpose* with Lori. We were both scheduled to leave Monday morning, but my flight was canceled before we even left for the airport. When I called the airline, I was informed that due to bad weather back home, it could take up to three days to get rebooked. What!?

I could feel panic rising in me. I had no place to stay (finding a last-minute hotel room in Manhattan would surely cost a fortune) and no one to pick up my kids after school. But that didn't matter to the ticket agent on the phone. In fact, she didn't seem to care at all. I didn't know what to do. Yell at her? Cry into my hotel pillow? And then it hit me: I could expect something good to come from it. In fact, maybe it had happened on purpose. With that thought, I could feel a shift in myself; the tension released and trust took its place.

"I'm just going to have faith this will all work out," I told the airline rep, who had been pressuring me to make a decision about the date I wanted to fly home. "So, I'll call you back after I've worked through some other details."

"Ma'am, the alternate flights will fill very fast," she argued. "If you wait, you might get stuck there longer or have to pay a large fee."

"It'll be okay; I've got really good angels," I told her. I hung up, took some deep breaths, and asked whoever was listening—God, Spirit, angels, loved ones—to work their magic and help me see the good in the situation.

Lori emerged from the bathroom, where she'd been packing up her things. "Everything okay?" she asked. I told her yes, that I trusted it would all get figured out after she left.

After hugging Lori goodbye and watching her cab speed off to the airport, I stopped at the hotel's front desk. There were no rooms available that night, the concierge told me. "But you could visit our VIP lounge while you sort things out," he said. "In fact, stay there all day if you'd like."

Up on the thirty-third floor, I discovered a gorgeous room with a breathtaking, wraparound deck overlooking Manhattan. Lori and I had stayed in that hotel for three nights and had no idea this little gem existed! And apparently, neither did anyone else; I had the place all to myself.

I made a couple of calls from the lounge and, like magic, everything was taken care of within thirty minutes. I got booked on a flight the next day, my in-laws used points from a rewards program to secure a hotel room for me, and my husband rearranged his schedule to be home for the kids after school.

Feeling so relieved, I stood there marveling at the panoramic view and perfect blue sky, grateful to have the entire space—and a whole day—to myself. Suddenly, I could hear the singsong chattering of Spirit swirling around me. They were ready to deliver their next message!

I grabbed my laptop and as soon as I sat down, something in the sky caught my eye and took my breath away. A little white feather danced above my head and landed at my feet. Thirty-three stories up, I had yet to see a single bird fly by. I took that little feather as a divine sign that I was right where I belonged.

As I dove into a full day of transcribing Spirit's words, I was surprised when they addressed me directly, revealing further insights about my altered travel plans. They made it clear that my getting "stuck" actually freed me up to work with them, uninterrupted and in a state of grace.

For a long time, Lori and I have trusted that the universe has been conspiring in our favor, buoyed by synchronicities like that magical day in New York. But the more we've honored and revealed our hidden truths—spiritual experiences and intuitive gifts we kept under wraps for years—the more we've noticed such magic appearing with great consistency in our lives. Reading through this next step, we realize this is no coincidence. Spirit wants it to be known that this is possible for anyone, especially for you. We can't wait to see your dreams come true. . . .

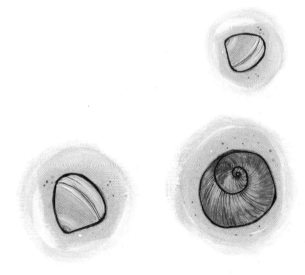

Dear Dreamer,

To hide your truth from anyone is to jeopardize enriching everyone

MESSAGE FROM SPIRIT

DOES IT FEEL AS THOUGH YOU HAVE SET SAIL FOR THE TRIP OF A LIFE-time? There it is, rising to the surface of you, the pull of purpose calling you forward. For centuries, voyageurs have trusted the mighty sea to deliver them from struggle and to reveal new lands of opportunity. You are the descendants of these explorers, navigators, visionaries, and adventurers. They are part of you, like stars in your night sky, and have called you here to brave the deep waters.

We understand your desire to steer the ship but respectfully request that you release your grip and follow our lead. In the light of your trust, we vow to hold your hand and steady your heart as you begin to embody your wildest dreams. The questions crashing into you, the doubts creeping up on you, and the inner voices mocking you are uninformed; they are incapable of honoring what is holy in you and what is wholly intended and possible for you.

You are in the arms of divinity when you allow for life to proceed within a timeframe orchestrated by the universe that supports you—rather than one defined by a society that pressures you to do more, have more, accomplish more, and fit in more.

Liv, your view from this rooftop is a bird's-eye view of all that is possible. We delight in you sharing the story of this act of divine timing with the magic makers gathered for this lesson, for it is just as much for them as it is for you, provided as an example of the ease with which you may move forward when you trust that the Powers That Be have ulterior motives.

You did not panic upon news of travel delays and flight cancellations. You continued to trust (as you have throughout the rapid creation of these teachings) that perhaps there were other forces at work and that perhaps you would be delivered to the perfect place—just not the place printed on your ticket.

The pieces fell into place quite effortlessly as soon as you requested divine intervention. Loved ones stepped in to handle the details, and strangers stepped in to help you feel safe and supported in an unknown place. This is the Call of the Wild, the voice that says, "Even if I am lost, I am already found." And now, here you sit, overlooking a busy world of comings and goings, elevated above the fray, separated from the chaos, with a panoramic view and a grateful heart.

This kind of view, this heightened awareness, this experience of living in awe of your own life is possible for each and every one of you reading this, each and every day.

At this point in your journey, it may feel far easier to be swept away by the pressure to perform and the expectation to conform. Consider your circles of influence: the peers with whom you congregate most, the family that shaped you, the colleagues who praise or criticize your work, and the acquaintances whose curious comments or digitized lives prompt you to question your worth in the world. How do these circles impact your way of being?

It pleases us to no end that as part of your attraction to these teachings, you join hands with a community of good-hearted artisans—makers, thinkers, and healers inspired in a multitude of ways to create and collaborate with Goodness. You might expect that we would advise you to *only* connect with those who see and honor the light in you, those with whom you are most comfortable and conscious. Indeed, these comrades are critical for your sense of belonging and your cultivation of joy. But teachers and givers appear in many forms.

The beauty of humankind and your place in it is that every interaction you experience with another human being is a stepping stone on your path. Rather than fume over tension, friction, and miscommunications, you can consciously redirect this energy and use it to propel you forward. When you see your past through the telescope lens of an open heart, you recognize how relationships fraught with tension and friction have informed your choices and perspectives, which impact your vocations, values, and spiritual evolution. They were not stumbling blocks after all, but life-shaping, view-finding opportunities to strengthen your resolve, clarify your priorities, and reveal your gifts.

You have worked, without anyone asking, insisting, or paying you, to alter behavioral patterns, heal from past wounds, address the source of traumas you've experienced, and express your rich and valuable perspectives through the creation of beauty and the reframing of your stories.

You must know, beloved, that the existence of trying relationships does not end with the bright-light revelations that come from stepping into the wild unknown and paving your path to purpose. Rather, this deepened commitment to living your truth softens the harshness of such interactions and allows you to take what you need from them, disregarding what does not serve the Highest Good for all involved.

We wish to share a story with you today.

Once, there was a man who lived by the sea. He lived a fair life with few grievances but little glory. One night, in a vivid dream, he was told of treasure to be found upon the shore. A messenger had come to him as he slept, cloaked in .velvet and dripping in jewels so shiny the man could almost see his reflection in them.

"Your path to riches will be a story of the ages," the messenger told him. "Go in the light of the rising sun, upon the shores of the rolling sea, and trust that buried treasure will reveal itself to you. You shall provide for your family in unimaginable ways and also enrich the lives of those you do not know."

As soon as he awakened, the man went to the sea and walked along its shore. For more than a year, this was his practice, in sunshine and rainstorms, to walk barefoot through deep sand, his head hung low as he scanned the ground for buried treasure. Every shell he found was empty, save for strings of seaweed and grains of sand. Every coin he spotted was rusted and worn, worth no more than face value. He kept walking and waiting and watching.

One day, his quiet walk at dawn was interrupted by an unfamiliar voice. He looked up to see a woman walking briskly toward him, waving wildly to get his attention.

"I have seen you out my window many mornings," she told him. "And I must know what it is you're looking for!"

The man felt panic rising in him. He could not tell this perfect stranger the nature of his pursuits, for she might begin looking, too, and steal his yet-unfound treasure. He had not even told his wife or daughters the real reason for his morning walks for fear that they might laugh at his dream or discourage him from continuing on. His dream was his secret, as was the treasure it promised.

"It is not for you to know," he told the woman and continued walking. She was not satisfied, for she was burning with curiosity and was now irritated by his secrecy. She pleaded with him,

insisting she was trustworthy. She followed behind him, guessing aloud what he was looking for. Something lost? Something living? Something ancient?

The more she talked, the more annoyed the man grew. "Leave me alone," he snapped. "Right now, all I want is some peace and quiet!"

This angered the woman, who wanted nothing more than to know his story. "If that is what you want," she replied, "and all I want to know is what you are looking for, then I'll walk with you and talk to you until you tell me! Once you do, I'll have my answer and will leave you here so you can have your peace and quiet."

The man walked for miles, and the woman kept pace. She talked while he fumed. Her voice cut through his concentration, her stories clouded his thoughts, and her opinions clashed with his own. He refrained from picking up shells or coins so as not to clue her in to his daily mission. He grew increasingly unfocused. Not only could he not pay attention to what was beneath his feet, but he felt hot in the sun and small beside the ocean. For the first time in all of his walks, he felt weary. Finally, he threw up his hands and shook his fist.

"You win! I cannot focus with you here," he said sternly to the woman by his side.

"Then tell me what it is you're looking for," she said eagerly.

"I'm searching for treasure," the man sighed and reluctantly told her of his dream and the message he'd received.

The woman hung on to his every word, fascinated by his story.

"But it could have simply been a figment of your imagination," she replied, wide-eyed. "Why did you believe the message?"

"Because I awakened with the power of it pulsing through me," he replied.

"So, you seek the unknown without fail, every day." The woman almost whispered this, entranced by the notion of it.

"I do . . . for what if the treasure appears on the day I give up?" The man noticed, as he spoke, that his fatigue was fading. Telling this perfect stranger about his dream and answering her questions stirred renewed energy in him.

"But isn't it monotonous," the woman asked, "to walk the same beach at the same time every day?" Her inquisitiveness seemed genuine, and the man could feel his prior irritation with her lifting from his heart.

"To the contrary," he replied. "Every walk is different. The sun never looks the same rising up over the sea, and every morning the sea places new sand beneath my feet. There are days when it feels a little like a dream, to be one with the sea and sky, to feel as though the birds are singing just to me. Even though I have not found my treasure, I feel richer for having taken the walk."

The woman stood in silence, soaking in his words. "Thank you for sharing it with me," she finally said. "I will cherish this walk with you."

"And I," the man said, "am pleasantly surprised I can say the same to you." And with that, the woman left the beach.

Standing in the peace and quiet, the man felt lighter some-how, as if a burden had been lifted from his shoulders. He headed home, emboldened by sharing his story with a perfect stranger, and promptly revealed to his wife the real reason for his walks at dawn. She did not laugh or scoff as he had feared, but encouraged him to continue. At least he was getting fresh air daily, she said, and at best, his dream might come true one day.

Weeks passed and the man continued his daily walks at sunrise alone until one morning, when he arrived at the beach just before dawn, he noticed the silhouettes of three boys standing near the sea. They ran toward him.

"Excuse me, sir," said one of the boys. "Are you the Dreamer?"

He was taken aback and looked at them quizzically.

The second boy asked, "Are you the man who follows his dream each day without fail?"

The man felt his heart skip a beat. "Perhaps," he said slowly, "but how could you know of me?"

"Everyone knows of you," the third boy answered enthusiastically. "We have all heard the story of the woman who walked with you once and was forever changed. She calls you the Dreamer and tells of your wisdom but not your whereabouts, so we have been searching for you!"

One of the boys held out a small bag. "We bring a small offering, hoping you might let us walk with you, too."

The man loosened the velvet cord which kept the cloth bag closed and peeked inside. There were two glistening coins, three fresh oranges, and a handful of sweets his children would love. Treasures! Sheer delight and awe pulsed through his veins, and he laughed out loud. He began to walk and gestured to the boys, inviting them to follow. The boys rushed to his side and showered him with questions as they walked through the sand, curious about patience and purpose, faith and dreams.

"We are rich!" they exclaimed at the end of the walk, delighted by the insights they had gained and eager to share with others. The man took the bag of treasures home and, quite amused by the way in which his dream had come true, told his wife what had happened. Over dinner that night, their family delighted in the small bag of treasures. "To following our dreams," the man said, raising his glass.

The next morning the man awakened before dawn, as had become habit for him. Instinctively, he headed down to the beach despite having already seen his dream come to fruition. When he arrived, he was surprised to find six people waiting on the beach, each carrying a knapsack of small treasures—jewels and gems, coins and treats. They walked with him as the awakening sky burned orange and sparkled lavender.

Each morning after, the crowd grew, following in the man's footsteps, listening to his stories, and offering tokens of their appreciation.

"We have more good fortune than I could ever have imagined," his wife gasped as he arrived home with more gifts. "What did you say to that woman that made such an impression?" she wondered.

"I do not know," he admitted. "I only shared the truth of my journey and the treasures I'd already found in it. In fact, I had been worried she would take my dream and run with it."

His wife smiled and said, "Well, thank Goodness she did."

We share this parable with you today to illustrate this, dear dreamer: to hide your truth from anyone is to jeopardize enriching everyone.

The Dreamer may not directly connect with every person on Earth, but by living in the light of his personal truth and remaining committed to the dream that birthed it, he contributes to elevating the consciousness of the planet. We invite you to see that the trailblazers you have walked alongside have done the same, positively altering the very vibration of humankind by giving voice to their visions.

This is a story about choices. The man you just read about was not desperate for money, for unending abundance. The promise of more than he already had was certainly motivating, as was the notion of impacting others in beneficial ways. The message he received stayed with him, moving from his subconscious into his conscious mind. It was too powerful for him to ignore. He awakened with the knowing that he must follow that guidance, that vision, even if he did not have the full picture. He did not need to know why or how, only that he had been chosen for this specific mission. He did not even know what he was looking for, so he focused on what felt most tangible: a search for buried treasure. Little did he know that truth revealed and wisdom gained were the real treasures of the story, as elusive as the closely guarded secret of his dream.

You can relate to this man, for you have received messages, visions, dreams, or ideas that guided you to follow something, to try something, or to explore something in the name of Everlasting Goodness. Have you ever had a dream that felt like it was real? Have you ever had a vision so vivid it followed you for days? Have you ever imagined an alternative reality that seemed so good you later longed for it?

The man in our story followed his dream and did as he was advised, but the reward of his efforts was long in coming for one reason: he kept it a secret. We desire for you to know and fully embrace this truth: when you give voice to a vision, its power and potential expands exponentially. We find that so many dreamers get distracted at this juncture. They may honor the dream, vision, or idea by holding it inside and remember-ing it daily, but they underestimate the detrimental effects of shrouding it in secrecy.

Everything is made of energy— you *and* the guidance you receive night and day. The vibrational frequency of inspiration is deadened in the darkness. In an effort to protect themselves from ridicule or jealousy, dreamers often opt to keep their grandest visions quiet, only to grow bitter or weary over hopes and dreams that never saw the light of day. What they do not realize is that divinely inspired dreams are never meant to be held and guarded, but to be set free.

The man in our story did not share his dream until he was given a choice: keep it secret and feel increasingly miserable, or tell it and be granted peace. The promise of contentment won over his heart and prompted him to reveal the truth. Quite rapidly he felt the tension in his body and the worry in his mind release. By letting his guard down and giving voice to that dream, he heard his own truth pouring out of him and the gifts of his walks revealed. His path to a higher purpose became evident, and the rewards of it—in all forms—exceeded the expectations of his own imagination.

This is, by far, the most powerful action you can take today to bring your visions to life and to turn your inspired thoughts into reality. Say them out loud to anyone and everyone. Discernment is not a virtue; assuming you know which people are safe to tell your stories to is just as dismissive of and detrimental to the expansive power of your path to purpose as hiding it from *everyone*. You cannot possibly know who is waiting in the wings to help propel you forward.

Is it possible that one or more people might deem your dream to be laughable or ludicrous? Of course, beloved. And what a gift they are, challenging you to recall the vividness and vibrancy of your vision, your sense of being called to something greater than yourself. When you are in the vortex of that vibration, the ego-based or low-energy responses to your vision are powerless. You receive the gift of clarity, free of charge.

And is it possible that one or more people might deem your dream to be meaningful and motivating? Of course, beloved. And what a gift *they* are, asking you to recall the vividness and vibrancy of your vision, your sense of being called to something greater than yourself. Once again you find yourself in the vortex of that vibration, and the heart-based or high-frequency responses to your vision are powerful. You receive the gift of clarity, supernaturally charged.

By repeating aloud to yourself and others that you are pursuing your passions, crystallizing your purpose, and trusting what comes, everything shifts within you and around you. If you feel you have shared some of this but still feel stuck, it is because you are still standing guard over some deeper truth or in certain company.

Please believe us when we say that the eight letters that spell out the word "universe" cannot come close to defining the infinite amount of support that is available to you in every single moment. When your earthly existence aligns with your soul's purest intentions and your planet's unmet needs, All of Existence delights in the sound of your voice.

When you stop pretending that you are less than the brilliance of your purpose and choose to follow that which your heart desires and which your dreams are calling you toward, this is what happens: you and your glorious mission on Earth become the center of the universe. Even if you don't know where you're going, you trust it's where you belong.

And so we ask you today to give voice to your visions, dear dreamer, whether undefined or detailed. You have a truth to share: you are stepping into the wild unknown not because you know what treasures you'll find there, but simply because it is calling you. Perhaps you have told almost no one this. Perhaps you have told only those you regard as "safe." Or perhaps you have shared pieces of your path to purpose with many, but not the truest, grandest, and most fantastically outlandish hopes that give you chills from head to toe. Ah, there are truths still to be told.

We now ask that you share your path to purpose with five people. In the coming days, you'll be presented with opportunities to follow your instincts and share what feels good at work, in your neighborhoods, in social settings, in classrooms, or in family forums. Begin with the words that make you the glorious and deserving center of the universe: *I AM.*

> *I am trying something new. . . .*
>
> *I am leaving behind what no longer serves me. . . .*
>
> *I am trusting the universe to. . . .*
>
> *I am honoring my gifts by. . . .*
>
> *I am feeling called to help. . . .*
>
> *I am ready to tell you who I really am, what I really desire, and what I really dream of doing. . . .*

The Powers That Be will rally around your Call of the Wild. With intergalactic Goodness working in your favor, there is absolutely no stopping you or your glorious mission of the heart. We would like you to imagine, to the best of your ability, every positive force in the universe coming together in harmony, in your honor, and in service to your mission. Angels singing, stars sparkling, tides turning, spirits dancing, Masters congregating, planets aligning, and the heart of your globe beating to the tune of you.

Can you feel the momentum, the vibration, and the undeniable magnificence of All of Creation marching toward meaningful manifestation in your honor? Feel the tension lift as the truth spills out. Notice clarity tapping you on the shoulder. Watch synchronicity swoop in and support you. The truth that you feel most nervous to tell is the truth that will set you free.

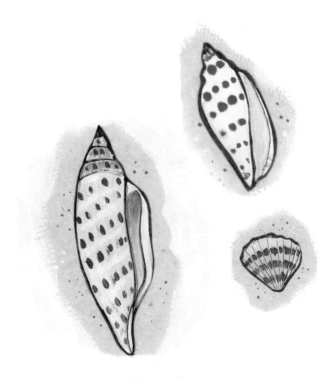

REFLECTION TWO

HERE I AM

IN THIS TEACHING, SPIRIT ASKS YOU TO REVEAL
YOUR PERSONAL TRUTHS AND EVOLVING DREAMS
TO FIVE PEOPLE. FIRST, IT'S IMPORTANT TO GET
CLEAR ON WHAT THOSE ARE AS YOU HONOR *WHO
YOU ARE*. BEGIN WITH THE "I AM" PROMPTS THAT
SPIRIT PROVIDED, IMAGINING YOURSELF SPEAKING
THESE WORDS TO SOMEONE, AND THEN EXPLAINING
HOW YOU ARE PERSONALLY AND AUTHENTICALLY
FOLLOWING THROUGH ON EACH STATEMENT.

I AM TRYING SOMETHING NEW. . . . *Share what it is and how you're doing it. Is it a new way of being? A new way of thinking? A new dream you're pursuing?*

....

....

....

....

....

....

....

....

....

I AM LEAVING BEHIND WHAT NO LONGER SERVES ME. . . . *Explain what this is and why you know it's time to let it go.*

....

....

....

....

....

....

....

....

....

I AM TRUSTING THE UNIVERSE TO. . . . *Complete the sentence, envisioning and explaining what you're ready to experience when feeling divinely supported.*

....

....

....

....

....

....

....

....

I AM HONORING MY GIFTS BY. . . . *First, allow yourself to see and celebrate your abilities—from the things people often compliment you on to the wisdom you have but may not always share. Then consider the ways you can reveal and/or deepen these talents, passions and traits.*

....

....

....

....

....

....

....

....

I AM FEELING CALLED TO HELP.... *Make note of the moments your heart aches for others, you feel compelled to contribute to a cause, or you have stood up for someone else. You might even connect the dots and notice a common thread through them all.*

....

....

....

....

....

....

I AM READY TO TELL YOU WHO I REALLY AM, WHAT I REALLY DESIRE, AND WHAT I REALLY DREAM OF DOING.... *Consider, as Spirit said, the truths you are most nervous to share and reveal them here.*

....

....

....

....

....

....

....

....

Now that these "I AM" statements are customized to reflect the real you, practice sharing them with others. As you do, list the five people you revealed your truth to and note how it felt.

1..

2..

3..

4..

5..

INSPIRING STORIES OF INFINITE PURPOSE

THE ART OF DREAMING BIG

When artist Susie Lubell first heard about *Infinite Purpose*, she was emerging from a chaotic period. Her family of five had just moved in the heat of summer to a new house near Jerusalem during a time of great political unrest—and then a war.

"Yes, I live where there are actual wars," she told us. "And I was hanging by a thread." Susie hoped that once things settled down and the kids returned to school, she'd find respite in her work again. But after several years of working full time as an artist, she'd grown bored with her artwork. She felt ready to experiment and potentially change her style and looked to Spirit's teachings to help reignite her creative fire.

"I just felt ready to explode with new energy," Susie said. "I was so ready for the words of Spirit that I felt they were spoken for me specifically, particularly the bit about telling your truth."

As she intuitively experimented with her art, creating large mixed media paintings with bold colors and whimsical folk imagery, she shared the new images online and revealed the truth about her biggest dreams. "I haven't been totally truthful about my professional aspirations," she bravely wrote on her blog. "I fear the kind of criticism and rejection that comes with sharing and achieving big dreams . . . [but] I just can't do it anymore. I can't be small. Being small serves no one. I'm big. Like a whale. And my aspirations are whale-sized, too."

She went on to share her visions of finding new audiences, being featured in art exhibitions all over the world, and teaching workshops in self-expression through painting. Soon after, an old friend she'd known since fourth grade reached out to ask if he could license twenty of her paintings—including her bold new artwork—for a puzzle app he'd developed. Susie excitedly agreed, and in the first two days, there were over 2,000 downloads. She received email after email asking where people could buy more of her "magical" and "mesmerizing" artwork. Holy wow!

"I felt I was on the right path toward sharing my vision and work with a wider audience," Susie said.

To watch Susie's dreams continue to come true, follow her online at susielubell.com.

RISING FROM THE ASHES

Amanda Fall was riding high when everything fell apart. "I thought I knew exactly who I was and where I was headed," she told us. After all, she'd spent the past three years making her lifelong dream a reality: publishing an indie digital magazine designed to be a place of hope and comfort for sensitive souls like herself.

But when her mother-in-law passed away unexpectedly at age fifty-seven, everything changed. Amanda, her husband, and their family felt crushed by grief and struggled to find a new normal.

"When I turned back to the place I normally found comfort, my magazine, something felt different there, too," Amanda said. "I felt constricted, unable to share my full story. I hid behind false smiles and 'everything-is-okay' when that was far from the truth."

Feeling deeply called to the teachings of *Infinite Purpose*, Amanda took Spirit's words to heart, inspired to share the stories of her grief more openly. And just as Spirit had promised, it set her free.

"As I aligned closer to my truth, I discovered something startling: this raw and real version of me felt more authentic, more vibrant, and more genuine than ever before."

And her readers responded in kind, which amazed Amanda. They felt honored by and grateful for her willingness to be vulnerable and give voice to the underbelly of grief. Amanda could feel something new stirring awake in her. She felt inspired to continue reaching people on a deeper, truer level—providing comfort, companionship, and light for their dark places.

"I was no longer the same, so my business couldn't be, either," Amanda said. "In the wake of grief, loss, and my aching heart seeking healing, I found our new identity, *The Phoenix Soul*. We rise from the ashes of doubt, fear, and regret. We unite in telling our vulnerable truths."

As she continued to walk through the teachings of *Infinite Purpose*, Amanda launched her new online magazine at thephoenixsoul.com to rave reviews.

"I am forever grateful to Liv and Lori as messengers of Spirit, for being there for me in a way I never expected, with joy and new life rising from the ashes of pain and death," she said. "We are all reborn, every day, into hope and newness, if we are willing to live our truth boldly."

STEP THREE

JOY RISING

ON CHRISTMAS MORNING IN 1985, FIFTEEN-YEAR-OLD LORI GAVE HER dad a sweatshirt for Christmas that said, *Best Dad on Earth*. It wasn't just a cliché; she meant it. Lori adored the way her dad's face lit up whenever she walked into a room, how he kept his cool when she made mistakes or had teen-age meltdowns, how he made her laugh, and how he always made her feel safe. Lori remembers her dad, who had been sick for four months, feebly pulling the sweatshirt out of the gift box and smiling. "I guess I can't get any better than that," he told her.

Two days later, Lori's dad died of cancer. She recalls that dark day so vivid-ly, from the sound of the zipper on the body bag to the desperation that over-whelmed her. For months, it felt like a cloud of sadness had permanently parked itself over her family's home and inside her heart. But one night, Lori was suddenly aware that her dad was standing in the hallway outside her bedroom. To this day, she doesn't know if she was dreaming or awake for his visit; it felt *that* real. She was so elated to see him, arms outstretched, looking healthy and happy.

"He told me he was doing great and that I could move on now," she recalls. And then Lori's dad told her he'd always be with her, even if she couldn't see him, that everything would be okay, and she could go back to bed.

"When I woke up the next morning," Lori says, "the heavy weight crushing my heart was lifted. It suddenly seemed like I was allowed to be happy again, know-ing he was around and wanted me to move forward." Lori still grieved deeply for her beloved dad, but sensing his presence throughout her life has brought great comfort.

In 2012, Lori's dad figured out he could communicate with her through *me*. One day while Lori and I were together, he showed up in spirit armed with lots of details for me to share with her, wanting to make sure she knew it was really him. Lori, as you might imagine, melted into a puddle of joyful tears. And I instantly fell in love with him. He was so darling, and I told him he could check in anytime.

He took me up on this offer. Ever since, he periodically shows up while I'm talking on the phone with Lori or even thinking about Lori. He appeared on the day before Thanksgiving in 2013 wanting to say hi to his "pumpkin pie." When I told Lori, she excitedly shared that this had been his nickname for her. Her dad then showed me images of greeting cards and hearts, which immediately reminded Lori of the many cards he had given her while she was growing up. "I'm sending her cards," he told me. We thought that was super sweet, but we didn't realize he was actually trying to get some cards to her.

A couple of weeks later, while looking for packed-away art supplies in her basement, Lori stumbled upon an old folder full of handmade cards *she* had made as a girl. "I had totally forgotten that when I was little I made greeting cards for my mom and dad for every birthday and holiday," she said. "I took it so seriously like it was my job, sure that I'd work for Hallmark some day. I even created a little logo on the backs like a 'real' card. It turns out my dad saved every one of them."

As Lori looked around her studio, surrounded by her actual line of greeting cards sold at stores around the world, her heart skipped a beat remembering how much joy card making had brought her as a little girl, realizing that childhood dream had come to fruition, and knowing how much her creations had meant to her dad. It all felt like validation that she was on the right path, purposefully using her gifts to bring joy to others.

We think it's the perfect example of what Spirit teaches in this next step. Hang on tight; you're in for the ultimate joyride. . . .

MESSAGE FROM SPIRIT

HAVE YOU EVER LOST SOMETHING AND SPENT A GREAT DEAL OF TIME and energy looking for it, in senseless *and* probable places, only to have it appear without explanation right in the place where you insist you looked a thousand times? Yes, of course. We have watched you do this with tension and frustration escalating not only over trivial items such as clothing and keys, but in your attempts to uncover the very essence of who you are and why you came here. Like a dog chasing its tail—amusing to watch, perhaps, but disorienting to be the chaser and the chased all at once.

So, you are searching under chairs and inside closets for your purpose? Convinced it is just around the corner and closer than you think? Have a seat, beloved. Cleanse your body and untangle your stories with a deep breath. And another. As many as you need. Please center yourself in preparation for the following truth.

IF YOU ARE LOOKING FOR YOUR PURPOSE, YOU WILL NEVER FIND IT.

Another breath, please.

Purpose is the positive energetic undercurrent of a life well lived, fuel for the fire within you that asks not just "how can I help?" but, more deliberately, "how can my joy be a light?"

Your purpose cannot be found as if it were a treasure buried in the sand. To search for your purpose is like blowing hot air into a balloon full of holes. There is so much displaced energy that leaves you feeling deflated and depleted, beloved. Your reasons for being do not exist outside of you; you must allow them to rise up from within you. Let us show you how.

First, feel joy.

Second, deepen joy.

Third, use the source of that joy as the source of your service.

You may be shocked and befuddled by how simple it sounds. We ask that you refrain from complicating matters by questioning the validity of this and poking more holes in your proverbial balloon. Before you deem this too uncomplicated for a human being to bear, too good to be true, we invite you to breathe in the truth of the matter.

We understand the desire to know where you're going and why you're going there; you have been conditioned to only move forward with these answers in hand. But we ask you, as we have before, to have faith in the small steps that lead to the big picture you speak of.

It is imperative that you understand that your purpose is not a singular pursuit, achievement, or mission. To search for one accomplishment or passion that defines your worth in this world is to discount all of the meaningful, influential, and inspired experiences of your journey thus far. What if they, too, were aligned with your purpose?

You were born into this world already knowing what it was you intended to accomplish in this lifetime, even if it required struggle, confusion, frustration, and a sense of disorientation. You had confidence that those so-called hardships would not do you in, but would reveal what you must do in order to create more light. It is not that you do not know your purpose, but simply that you have forgotten it along the way, so much so that you may not even recognize it when you're standing in it. Rather than call yourself incompetent, please call yourself *incredible*—for you are here now because of where you've been and because All of Creation believes in you. What you perceive as missteps are, in fact, divine distractions and scenic detours. The universe recalibrates with every choice you make,

beloved, to ensure that the invitation into deeper joy is always within your reach.

Let us return to the notion of losing something valuable to you, like the keys to a door
you feel you must access. Have you seen
the pattern in your life that goes like this: you
realize the keys are missing, you look for them
without success, you begin to panic and watch the
clock, you begin to imagine the worst case scenarios,
and then, as if by some miracle, the keys reveal themselves to
you? Sometimes, the problem is solved when someone tells you where they are
or you take a moment to center yourself and retrace your steps. In some cases,
you ask for divine intervention and receive it promptly. But sometimes you take
matters into your own hands and have new keys made, only to later find the original set and shake your head at the energy, time, and money spent on creating a
backup.

We see, time and time again, this scene play out as you look for your purpose,
half expecting to find it sitting at the Lost and Found looking fed up and forlorn.
It is undeniably deflating to stand before a door you need to open, you *want* to
open, and to realize you don't know how to get in. You may feel more productive
and distract your mind from its frustration by launching into desperate action—
make new keys, kick down the door, climb through a window, and open it from the
inside. When you get the door to open, you are already exhausted. Meanwhile,
you might have achieved the same result simply by standing, waiting, and trusting
the door would somehow open for you at the perfect time as determined by the
universe that is, as you rightly believe, conspiring in your favor. Help would appear,
or the keys would turn up just in time. You would walk through the door feeling not
exhausted, but exhilarated by the obvious synchronicity of it, the clear invitation

to walk right in.

This is not to say *do not take action*. This is to say *do not take action that is motivated by desperation*, by wanting, by impatience.

Those of you convinced that time is running out have it backwards, for in this belief, you are turning your back on time.

Those of you convinced that someone will fill your shoes if you do not act swiftly are answering your divine calling with fears of competition and scarcity, resulting in a compromised connection to Wonder.

Those of you who believe there are not enough material rewards to compensate for following your heart are blocking the flow of abundance into your life, as if telling your bank to be suspicious of any deposits that come from benevolent people and places.

And to those of you who continue to tell the story to yourself and others that your reason for being is smaller than, less illustrious than, less impressive than, or less influential than most others', we say this to you with love: *enough*.

Imagine a child who receives good marks on her assignments but argues with the teacher that she does not deserve such accolades because her fellow students' work looks different from her own. What sense is there in this? What a loss for humanity if this student insists on undermining her worth rather than allowing others to benefit from the way she sees the world and approaches her work. *Enough,* we say. You would not be here in this space, called to these teachings, if you were not aware at some level that you are, indeed, enough and prepared to step deeper into enlightenment.

We invite you to look at the horizon in Lori's artwork. Each one of you will notice something different. Some will first notice colors; others will notice details.

Some will count the layers; others will see no separation between the mountains, the grass, and the sky. There is no right way to see it and interpret it.

Here is where your eyes will meet: none of you can know definitively what is *beyond* that horizon. Will that keep you from exploring it, or will the lighthearted, light-filled, richly colored landscape be enough to invite you in? Perhaps you say, "Yes, let's explore!" but then feel tension rise up with your next thought: "But, how?"

"It looks a long way off," you might say.

"It looks like an arduous climb," you might say.

"It looks as if there may not be civilization to support us," you might say.

"It looks far from home and may not be worth the trek," you might say.

"It looks like Home to me, and that is as scary as it is exciting," you might say.

"I want to see more, but I have no idea how or where to begin," you might say.

We hear you. We understand this horizon is different from anything you've seen before, any scenic view you've driven by. It is vibrationally different, and you can feel it, for you have been changed already and see your own horizon with new eyes. The shifts taking place within you, even as you ask the questions of "how" and "when" and "why" and "why me," are reorganizing priorities within you, renewing your sense of Self and revealing the original intention with which you entered this lifespan, this unpredictable journey to unshakeable and unconditional joy.

If purpose is the undercurrent in the river of your life, joy is the water. Neither exists without the other.

Many use the words joy and happiness interchangeably, but they are not one and the same. Joy is the highest frequency of existence. It is the exaltation that results from consciously pointing your personal compass toward heartfelt gratitude, soul fulfillment, authentic expression, pure love, deep faith, spiritual connection, and inner peace. When molecules of joy make up the water of your river, you flow through life's challenges and choices with greater ease and certainty. Indeed, deep-seated joy makes it possible to walk through grief with Grace, to address adversity with Hope, to feel safe even in dark corners, to be buoyed by laughter, to catch glimmers of magic even in misery, and to see the light in everyone, including, and especially, in you.

And this is why we ask you today, beloved, to shift your focus from searching for your purpose and, rather, make it your mission to cultivate Joy in your life. Not just now and then, not only when you perceive things to be "going well", but in every moment. *Make joy the breath of you.*

We invite you now to recall a moment in your life when you wondered if, perhaps, you were exhibiting or tapping into your purpose. A conversation that helped another, a request for your good advice, a compliment that touched you, a thank-you that surprised you, a connection that felt destined, or a realization of a gift you possess. Remember that? It could have been ten years ago; it could have been today; it might have happened once or many times. Place yourself in that moment, see your surroundings, and feel your feelings; notice who else has been touched by this moment and by your presence.

Notice joy there, bubbling up to the surface of you. Perhaps it was fleeting, but it felt like everything was aligned in you and around you and that all was right with the world. There were no distractions, no doubts, and no worries because you were fully present, divinely guided, and living *on purpose*. Do not say you do not know this. Do not say it didn't matter. Do not cheat yourself and the world around you by falling back into that tired debate with scarcity. *Enough*, remember? It is, you are, we promise . . . *enough*.

Joy is the key to the door that stands before you. You are most needed where you are deeply moved. You are meant to give the gifts of which you have an endless supply. You are most productive when the "work" is so meaningful to you and delightful for you that it feels practically effortless and undeniably energizing.

Time is of the essence, meaning that we urge you to place immediate priority on that which feels aligned with the very essence of you—that which brings you deep, abiding joy. Perhaps you have found yourself in the business of saying yes to countless needs expressed, agreeing to acts of service that do good in the world but do not feel electrifyingly good to you. Entire organizations and movements have been built by people who did good to look good but have crumbled or become corrupt in the absence of genuine, soul-stimulating joy.

Of course, there is Good in all good works. But it is when joy is the passageway—the sparkling water that keeps divinity afloat—that the universal impact of those good works, of service to Self and others, accelerates and amplifies miraculously. In the light of joy, every act of Goodness gains momentum fueled by passion, innovation, and soul recognition. Your heightened vibration activates synchronicity, divine protection, and angelic intervention. You wouldn't try to make an electronic device work without plugging it into its power source, correct? Then why try to embody your perceived purpose without plugging into the source of your joy?

We find that makers, healers, and thinkers often stop short of tapping into this power source, assuming that because they enjoy what they do, they have found their purpose. Realizing a vocation or pastime through which you are able to channel the light of All That Is Good brings greater relief and gratification than other endeavors, indeed. The unique talents and personality traits you possess, a combined result of your soul path *and* life path, make you best suited for and delighted by certain professional and personal activities. This is a magnificent discovery, and many of you have made "doing what you love" a way of living or a goal for the future.

But even those pursuits can lose their luster if you feel directionless. The satisfaction you gain from *using* your gifts is compromised and jeopardized when they are not leveraged to propagate absolute joy. The positive impact and expansion of your chosen endeavors and amusements—such as writing, sculpting, nursing, sewing, inventing, advocating, teaching, healing, and performing—dramatically increase when tied to an enlightened level of joyful engagement.

Regardless of your talents and expertise, what elicits deep joy in you? Do you know? We invite you to jot down "joy notes," reflecting on the moments when you experience what we revealed earlier as signs of joy at work: heartfelt gratitude, soul fulfillment, authentic expression, pure love, deep faith, spiritual connection, and inner peace. May your laughter be amplified, may your interactions feel blessed, may you feel your heart swell with contentment, and may you notice when you feel magnetically drawn to certain topics of conversation, fields of interest, opportunities to help, and particular people. These are not mindless or frivolous uses of your time. Each one is an invitation to expand and for the joy in you to illuminate Goodness for others.

We are speaking to the artist who has worked hard to feel accomplished but longs to reveal the art that comes *through* her rather than the art that others have said would sell well. We are speaking to the writer who expertly crafts children's stories but feels most alive when comparing notes with peers on the grown-up magic in their midst. We are speaking to the cubicle dweller whose best moments at the office take place in her daydreams. We are speaking to all of you who are in the throes of moving, from getting by to flying high, from secret hopes to empowering truths.

These are important shifts happening in waves to all of you. Know that purpose shows up when you least expect it, right when you're immersed in joy, and asks to be included. You see it when art heals, when healing transforms, when performers transcend time and space, when words become wings, when services feel sacred, when conversations spark connections, when teachers inspire, and when parents model unconditional love. It is in this portal of All-Is-Possible that purpose is realized. Not found, but felt. Not discovered, but revealed. Not thought of, but intuitively *known*.

Radiate joy, beloved, and purpose will find you.

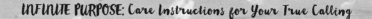

REFLECTION THREE

FOLLOW THAT JOY!

YOU ARE NOW ON A MISSION TO FIND JOY IN YOUR LIFE—FIRST IN THE *PAST* AND NEXT IN YOUR *NOW*. IN THIS CHAPTER, SPIRIT HAS ASKED THAT YOU RECALL A TIME WHEN YOU FELT JOYFULLY PURPOSEFUL, DEEPLY ENGAGED, FOCUSED ON *FEELING* GOOD AND *DOING* GOOD.

Spirit's examples included "a conversation that helped another, a request for your good advice, a compliment that touched you, a thank-you that surprised you, a connection that felt destined, or a realization of a gift you possess." It doesn't have to be life changing. In Lori's case, it was creating sweet cards for her parents. Use the space below to write down a time or two when you felt joyfully engaged in exploring, creating, or experiencing something good. What felt so great about it?

Now, turn your attention to today. Use the sheet below to jot down "joy notes" as Spirit instructed—moments of "heartfelt gratitude, soul fulfillment, authentic expression, pure love, deep faith, spiritual connection, and inner peace." Date each experience and share as much detail as you can so you can revisit for reminders of joy at work in your life.

WHAT BROUGHT YOU JOY? ....
WHEN DID IT HAPPEN? ....
EXPLAIN: ....

WHAT BROUGHT YOU JOY? ....
WHEN DID IT HAPPEN? ....
EXPLAIN: ....

WHAT BROUGHT YOU JOY? ....
WHEN DID IT HAPPEN? ....
EXPLAIN: ....

WHAT BROUGHT YOU JOY? ....
WHEN DID IT HAPPEN? ....
EXPLAIN: ....

*Pssst! See any connections or themes in your
reflections on joy between your past and today?*

INSPIRING STORIES OF INFINITE PURPOSE

LEARNING TO LAUGH AGAIN

When Lindsay Walz was a young girl, she was known for her infectious laugh. She remembers giggling so hard at times that she'd fall over in drunken delight. "But then the ground fell," Lindsay told us. "And with it went my joyful spirit."

In 2007, Lindsay was driving across the I-35W bridge in Minneapolis when it collapsed at the height of rush hour, sending her car and many others tumbling into the Mississippi River. Thirteen people died in that tragedy, and no one can explain how Lindsay made it out alive.

She emerged from the river broken—not just physically, but emotionally. Lindsay's infectious laugh was all but gone. "Feeling joy felt like a betrayal to the ones who were lost, who I thought could never feel joy again."

Lindsay made it her mission to make her life mean something, turning an old dream into a reality. Passionate about art and empowering youth, she launched a nonprofit called courageous heARTS to help kids discover, heal, and strengthen their hearts through creativity. Though the organization does wonderful work, creating it didn't heal her emotional wounds the way she'd hoped. It took some time and lots of inner work to realize that building courageous heARTS was as much a response to her survivor's guilt as it had been a source of joy.

"I wanted to prove to the universe that I was worthy of that next breath," she said.

Lindsay came to *Infinite Purpose* hoping to deepen her understanding of why she's here. She had thought creating courageous heARTS was the one and only reason her life was spared but now understands it's just one part of her life's purpose. In fact, to live her life *without* joy, she now sees, would be the real betrayal to those who lost their lives in the bridge collapse.

"I've grown to understand that living from joy, for joy, and with joy *is* my purpose. Sometimes that means shifting gears, changing perspectives, letting go, and sometimes it just means giggling again." To learn more about Lindsay and courageous heARTS, visit lindsaywalz.com or courageous-hearts.org.

HEALING WITH JOY

When Zina Canton began reading *Infinite Purpose*, she already knew she was ready for change. A self-proclaimed seeker, she'd felt out of sorts for some time, disconnected from her divine path.

"All the seeking that I'd done for years was an effort to outrun my pain," she said. "I spent decades of my adult life depressed, self-loathing, and suicidal. Even with all the workshops, meditation, talk therapy, reading, and praying, I was just barely living."

As she stepped into *Infinite Purpose*, Spirit's teachings cracked her wide open, she said, as she tearfully realized how deeply she'd been craving joy. Zina began to closely examine the deeply ingrained beliefs that were holding joy at bay, including the emotional scars of an abusive childhood. Zina worked to release beliefs about needing to "suck it up" when life got hard and that she was sensitive to a fault. As she let go of those old beliefs and traumas, she began to feel joy rising.

"I promised myself a different future and that it would not take a long, drawn-out process to get there," she said. "And I told myself there *would* be joyful moments along the way. That felt like a big promise to make."

To Zina's surprise, she began to notice joy showing up—from singing in the car to cooking one of her mom's recipes—and she started to write down each instance. Seeing each joyful moment on paper helped her to hold on to that emotion, to see proof of it emerging in her daily life, and to begin to dream even bigger.

"Just because things happened in the past didn't mean I couldn't trust that my future could and would be different," she said. This was a monumental shift for Zina. With that new level of courage, and using joy as her guide, she experienced rapid spiritual expansion. Messages began arriving in her dreams, her meditations provided deep and lasting healing, and she began to recognize and utilize some of her own spiritual gifts.

Now a certified life coach, Zina said the ways *Infinite Purpose* opened her up to joy and, in turn, her most purposeful path, have greatly enhanced her work with clients and allowed her to believe in her own bright future. Learn more about Zina at zinacanton.com.

STEP FOUR

THE POWER OF THE NIGHT SHIFT

DURING THE EIGHT WEEKS I RECEIVED AND TRANSCRIBED THE ORIGINAL *Infinite Purpose* teachings, with Lori adding Spirit's words to each sacred painting, we got into a pretty good rhythm. The message and artwork would be completed each Friday afternoon, ready to be emailed to participants the next morning. But everything went haywire as we prepared to share this fourth step.

For starters, it was a holiday week, so our schedules were thrown off. With my kids home from school and family gatherings added to the mix, I had less time than usual to receive the message. Spirit was patient with me as I transcribed their words little by little, day by day. But on Friday, I knew the message wasn't complete. We had family plans all day and didn't get home until evening, so I sat down to transcribe the rest of Spirit's teaching after the kids went to bed. As I sat there, my eyelids grew heavy and my mind started to wander. I was exhausted. Knowing Spirit's teaching was all about the power of rest, the irony of my fatigue wasn't lost on me!

I decided to take Spirit's advice, sure that after some good sleep, I'd be better equipped to receive their message in the morning. First, I decided to embed Lori's latest painting into the class email. I usually waited to do this step until the message was complete, but I figured it would be good to have that done before the morning, given the time crunch I was in. But there was a technical glitch; I couldn't even see the painting Lori had sent to me, and there was no way to download it. I emailed Lori, figuring she'd resend the image in the morning.

I went to sleep with the alarm clock set on my cell phone. I do this every night, and I'm never aware of texts or emails arriving. But in the deep of the night, I was pulled out of dreamland, aware of several faint "dings" coming from my phone. I ignored them, choosing to sleep. But a few minutes later, my phone buzzed louder and my eyes flew open. Was someone trying to reach me?

It was Lori, who had just sent me a text. I looked at the clock. It was a little before three a.m. my time, almost four a.m. for Lori. I texted her back: "What are you doing up!?" Lori replied that her hubby, Jay, had gotten up in the night, which was so unusual that it woke *her* up. But she couldn't get back to sleep; she had a haunting feeling that she needed to check her email. When she saw my message, she got up to resend the image, and then she sent me a text to let me know she'd fixed the glitch.

We exchanged a few messages, then texted each other good night. I closed my eyes, happy to go back to sleep. But right away, I heard Spirit's voice. "There is more," they said. "You were too tired before, and we have come to finish the message."

I tried to ignore them, but they persisted. Suddenly, I remembered a crucial piece of the message they'd already delivered about the divine guidance that can come deep in the night during the "sacred hours." I rose and realized I felt renewed and alert, even as everyone else in my corner of the world slept. I transcribed the rest of Spirit's fourth teaching in the still of the night. Then, I fetched Lori's gorgeous painting, ready and waiting for me since she, too, had been awakened in the night.

Lori and I don't think it's a coincidence we were both awakened to complete this particular message. Spirit's insights have deepened our understanding of the role that rest plays in our dance with the Divine while also opening our eyes to the inspiration that can come before the sun rises. We think of this next step as a wake-up call for all of us.

Awakening requires rest

MESSAGE FROM SPIRIT

TODAY, PERHAPS AGAINST YOUR WISHES, WE ASK THAT YOU LEARN TO rest. This guidance is not, as you might assume, antithetical to the purposeful joy you've been exploring and the positive momentum you've been feeling, but a critical step in the expansion of your light. Many of you are energized by your adventures in joy-finding, and this delights us. Some of you feel disoriented by pursuing joy, and we understand this.

Joy is not for the faint of heart. It is not a fleeting amusement, but meant as an everlasting state of being, which requires dedication and fortitude, particularly when professing misery is quite popular and when seemingly joyless challenges arise. Whether you are enthusiastically engaged in the cultivation of personal joy or, conversely, still unsure of what gives you great joy, either experience can be draining. And we ask that you honor this and treat yourself with loving care.

Fatigue expertly obstructs the vibrational flow between your spiritual Self and your physical self. Every part of your earthly being strives, in desperation, to achieve serenity (unaware that serenity is not an achievement, but a divine outcome of allowing). Have you seen a dog's ears perk up when he suspects something good is coming, such as the promise of a treat or a walk? He cocks his head slightly, on high alert, excited to be noticed and eager to receive.

You are not so different, are you? When you are in a state of unconscious desperation, your body tense with need, you place yourself on high alert—ears perked up in hopes that something good is coming. You are determined not to miss a critical piece of advice or a once-in-a-lifetime opportunity, so you keep your eyes open, barely blinking, and stay painfully focused on *not* missing what you've determined you're currently lacking and desperately need.

Do you remember our mentioning the absurdity of a dog chasing its tail? You know it all too well, correct? Round and round you go, ready to pounce, chasing a dream, an ideal, a conviction, or an ever-changing target. When you run in circles and finally stop, you cannot help but be so dizzy that you see a million paths before you. You crumple to the ground, lamenting the realization that even on high alert, fiercely focused, you cannot seem to find your way. "What is wrong with me," you shout to the heavens. "What must I do to turn confusion into clarity?"

There is nothing wrong with you, beloved. There is everything right with you. But to see this for yourself—to see the possibilities sprouting up in the wild unknown—will require a shift, a centering, a letting go. Awakening requires rest.

When darkness falls, as it does at the end of each day, lights turn on across the land. *Blink. Blink. Blink.* From our vantage point, those little lights ripple across your perpetually-in-motion planet as each person takes the same action—flipping a switch, pulling a string, or striking a match to turn on your lights, illuminating where you are on the inside as the outside falls away. We see you, nestled in your homes for the night, settling in and breathing easier after another busy day, wondering where the hours went, hoping for calmer waters tomorrow and a chance to make headway on the things that matter. And then you will try to do what you have been told to do: go to sleep.

Throughout your life, you have been informed, quite regularly, of the medical and scientific importance of getting "enough" sleep. There are guidelines, in fact, for the number of hours children and adults should sleep. Surely you've lived enough years here to know that no two babies require the exact same amount of sleep before they're each hungry or ready to play. Most babies arrive knowing innately when to sleep, wake, eat, and grow on their own timetable. But they learn, rather swiftly, that this is not the way of the world they have just joined. There are set times for eating and sleeping, working and playing (and playing is, most certainly, pushed further down on the priority list with every passing year).

But this rigid structure does not work for all, for you have your own, distinct circadian rhythms. You can sense intuitively, mentally, and physically when you are well rested and when you are not. Rather than focusing on the quantity of sleep you're getting, we suggest looking at the quality of sleep instead and its role in your life's calling.

There are advantages to structured routines, to be sure, but they leave little room for divinity. We know of the rat race, the daily grind, and the desire to get ahead and how it curiously and consistently leaves you feeling hopelessly behind, out of touch with the core of you. Is it any wonder you tire easily and struggle to feel energized? You stay up late or wake up early (and perhaps both) to get it all done. You run yourself ragged to do all you can. You eat on the go, talk on the go, squeeze all you can into a day, and then push yourself to do more.

When your body resists, you're not likely to nurture it, but to fight back; ignore it, debate it, drown it, sugar-coat it, medicate it, move it against its will, and even despise it. How often have you done everything but listened to your wise body? How frequently are you honoring the miraculous vessel that it is, complete with warning signs of physical unrest?

Night after night, so many of you wrestle with the gift of sleep. Some of you slam into it, so exhausted from the day's exploits that you crawl into bed half-conscious. Soon, you're walking through your days half-conscious, too. Some of you numb yourselves to sleep, needing voices, white noise, or medicinal aids to distract your active mind. Soon, you're walking through your days half-numb, too. Some of you rock yourselves to sleep, tossing and turning in the wake of fear, stress, and physical pain, eyes wide open as you finally shut down. Soon, your days feel unsettled, too.

WHAT WE NEED FOR YOU TO REALIZE IS THAT HOW YOU SLEEP IS HOW YOU LIVE.

So, we ask you today to begin examining your sleep, your quest for rest, through new eyes—the getting into it and the living into it. What awaits you on the other side of wakefulness, of consciousness, will often give you the creative fuel and light-filled strength you need for the day ahead, for your most purposeful path. You need not know precisely what it was and whom you saw as you slept. Just the sense each morning that you've come from dreamland to make good on a promise or to find good in your midst is enough.

To encourage the cultivation of a rich dream life and the deep rest that accompanies it, we invite you to approach sleep without fear or exhaustion, honoring it as not only a physical need, but as a spiritual necessity. Set aside the distractions that often accompany you at night—from fearful thoughts to glowing screens—and invite deep sleep to move through you. Not the altered state brought on by sleep aids and numbing agents, not the desperate state brought on by exhaustion, and not the state of simply wanting to escape a life burdened by acute stress.

What needs to change in order for you to routinely feel well rested? It would be our pleasure to assist you.

As you prepare your body for slumber, breathe in deeply, aware that you are easing into a meditative state. Notice every glorious inch of you—your toes, your heels, and your ankles—all the way up to the crown of your head. Eyes closed and body relaxed, recall three good things about your day. And then ask, silently or out loud, for sleep that guides you and energizes you to experience joy, make positive choices, and see the Divine at work in your life. If you can stay awake and aware

long enough to reflect on and invite in Goodness, you are more likely to awaken with a rested heart and renewed spirit, ready to embrace and embody your infinite purpose.

Your body is sacred, a work of art like no other. And it longs to collaborate with your mind and spirit so that you can go where you need to go, see whom you need to see, and walk where you need to walk on *purpose*. It was perfectly crafted to be the vehicle by which you reach your dreams, asleep and awake.

There will be times, indeed, when your dreams cross over into your earthly reality with vivid memories as you awaken. How fantastic this is, to break your barrier of time and space and bring a souvenir back from your adventures in the Great Beyond! Rather than ask everyone under the sun what these specific dreams mean, or try with no luck to decipher a message in a dream, pay attention to the *emotions* these dreams have triggered in you.

Your dreams are like messages from your Higher Self, created in cooperation with the universe to validate your deepest feelings and serve as trusted guides. There is a language barrier between your conscious and subconscious. Though the two understand each other perfectly in a dream state, as soon as you open your eyes in the morning, your mind jumps in to decipher the dream as best it knows how.

The dreams that matter most for your journey here, the ones that come with messages important for your path, work their way from obscurity into the spotlight of your soul. You may not even recall the specifics of the dream, but you'll know you've had one. You can feel it. Even if you cannot remember a single detail, you have the sense you traveled somewhere else in the deep of the night. Trust in that and hold it close, knowing the universe is working its magic, downloading new information, even as you sleep.

And throughout your day you may find yourself inexplicably approaching challenges differently, feeling joy rising up in you and feeling more deeply connected to that which you cannot see. This is due, in part, to an awe-worthy awareness that you somehow exist in and are engaged in realms beyond this earthly one, subconsciously collaborating with the Wonder of All. It is also due to you intentionally finding your way into restful sleep, the kind that refreshes your earthly body while you allow the rest of you to be immersed in divinely guided dreams.

Rather than obsessively interpreting the details of your dreams, unless they are very vivid and memorable in your waking hours, place the emphasis on how you felt in them. Trust the emotions that ride the wave with you from subconscious to conscious, and be aware of the ways in which they are reflected in your daily life.

For instance, if you wake up in a cold sweat, terrified of something in your dream, take note of where in your life you feel the equivalent. This is your Higher Self, in concert with the universe, alerting you to a mirrored experience in your waking hours. Act accordingly to release the experience or thought patterns producing this fear. The same is true of dreams that leave you feeling joyful, or reconnected to a loved one, or deeply engaged in following someone or something. Rather than work to release these positive experiences and thought patterns, know that you are being encouraged to cultivate and expand upon them. All in the name of Joy.

When your body is routinely feeling well rested, there will be nights when you awaken in the dark, in the early hours of the morning, as if someone has nudged you to get up. You may be inclined to turn over and go back to sleep, but notice how conscious you are, likely even more awake than when you groggily open your eyes in the light of day. These are the sacred hours, when the fog between here and there lifts. If you are awakened at this time while the masses sleep, know that you have been invited, divinely chosen, to take part in a gathering of inspired dreamers. The world around you is eerily and beautifully still with no noise or commotion to disrupt the open line of inspiration and divine communication. It is not unlike the inspired moments you have experienced while alone in nature or standing beneath running water in the flow of a stream of divine consciousness.

In the deep of the night, most human beings are in an elevated state, free of ego chatter and mind matter. This results in a clear energy field around you. There is no pressure to do anything, though it's a perfect time to invite the Divine to work through you. Should you be awakened while your corner of the world sleeps, most often between two and four o'clock in the morning, we encourage you to simply trust what comes, focusing only on feeling and receiving glorious guidance and divine protection. Carry this with you as you move into your days, likely more energized by the quiet inspiration that came to you in the still of the night.

IT IS IMPOSSIBLE TO SLEEPWALK THROUGH YOUR LIFE WHEN YOU'VE BEEN AWAKENED.

This teaching does not apply only to sleep, but to moving through your days in an awakened, enlightened state of being. When you grow physically fatigued, you complain that you have low or no energy. Unlike the positive physical sensations you experience when you are in the flow of All That Is Good (from buzzing to butterflies to a sense of no time passing), you experience physical deprivation in the wake of unrest. You move into a subconscious fight for survival. You forget how to trust. You forget how to move (thus, the frequent complaint of feeling stuck). You forget how to be.

Joy becomes elusive and your sense of purpose scurries back into hiding. Neither cares to be caught in the crossfire of a senseless war raging inside you, a battle you may not even be consciously aware of. You feel restless, unsettled, and on edge, but you're not sure why. Your ego wants you to believe that everything is falling apart so that it can take center stage again. It will warn you of what to worry about and reveal the "injustices" of your life—for your own good, it will claim—and cast doubt upon the steps you've taken to grow.

When you are tired of thinking and creating and doing and reacting, you're much like a newborn who is overtired and overstimulated. You fight the rest you need and do everything you can to keep your eyes open, to stay falsely present. *I cannot possibly rest,* you say, *because there's just too much to do.* We need for you to know that *constant* creation is not *conscious* creation. Your society places value on those who are driven, regardless of whether they are actually asleep at the wheel, filling the emptiness they feel (but do not dare speak of) with money rather than meaning, motivated to crush the competition rather than create Goodness. Their emotional intelligence and spiritual connections are compromised by chronic fatigue. They make rash decisions, expect immediate results, define success in numbers, and prefer small talk to soul talk. There is little room for interpretation and little time for inspiration.

But do not be fooled by your ego, which tells you *they* have it all wrong and *you* have it all right. It is far easier to cast blame and pass judgment than to see aspects of their stories reflected in your own. Know that we would not be addressing the importance of rest if we were not keenly aware of your need for it. We have not been fooled, nor has your spirit, by your attempts to look as though you are at peace when you are actually waging wars within, sitting quietly while inner chaos brews, breathing deep and holding it, hurriedly crafting your next great idea, numbing rather than nourishing your soul.

You are meant to feel comfortable and at peace in your body (not because of how you've perfected it, but simply because it is yours). You are meant to be keenly aware of how it speaks to you and committed to listening carefully to it, from aches of illness to sparks of intuition. You are meant to be well rested so that you may thrive in a state of well-being, effortlessly practicing purpose-magnifying patience, compassion, and gratitude. You are not meant to do everything, but to prioritize meaning-making and light-creating over all else.

We come to you now, wrapping you in a blanket made of stars. We are holding you close so you may rest your weary head upon us, feel the heartbeat of the universe pulsing through you, hear the music of Gentle Mercy flowing into you, sense the eyes of awestruck angels watching over you, experience the all-encompassing peace of a cradled newborn who is well nourished and well loved. May you rest in the knowing that the chase is over, that the tired days are behind you, that the dizziness of a million paths is no more.

You are awakening with new eyes to the glory of you, the power of your dreams, and to your enlightened path to purpose.

SLEEP AID

SPIRIT TELLS US "HOW YOU SLEEP IS HOW YOU LIVE" AND OFFERS TO HELP US HEAL THE HABITS THAT COMPROMISE THE ENRICHING REST OUR BODIES, MINDS, AND SPIRITS REQUIRE. EACH NIGHT FOR THE NEXT WEEK, FOLLOW SPIRIT'S INSTRUCTIONS (BOLDED BELOW) AS YOU CLIMB INTO BED. EACH MORNING, GIVE YOURSELF A MINUTE TO RECORD YOUR EXPERIENCE.

BEFORE YOU GO TO SLEEP:

- **NOTICE** every glorious inch of you—from your toes, your heels, and your ankles all the way up to the crown of your head.

- **RECALL,** with eyes closed and body relaxed, three good things about your day.

- **ASK,** silently or out loud, for sleep that guides you and energizes you to experience joy, make positive choices, and see the Divine at work in your life.

MORNING REFLECTIONS:

Today's Date: **Last Night's Bedtime:**   **Wake Up Time:**

Name three good things about yesterday that you were grateful for last night:

....

....

....

....

Notes on how you feel/what you notice:

....

....

....

Today's Date: **Last Night's Bedtime:**   **Wake Up Time:**

Name three good things about yesterday that you were grateful for last night:

....

....

....

....

Notes on how you feel/what you notice:

....

....

....

Today's Date: **Last Night's Bedtime:**   **Wake Up Time:**

Name three good things about yesterday that you were grateful for last night:

....

....

....

Notes on how you feel/what you notice:

....

....

....

Today's Date: **Last Night's Bedtime:**   **Wake Up Time:**

Name three good things about yesterday that you were grateful for last night:

....

....

....

Notes on how you feel/what you notice:

....

....

....

Today's Date: **Last Night's Bedtime:**   **Wake Up Time:**

Name three good things about yesterday that you were grateful for last night:

....

....

....

Notes on how you feel/what you notice:

....

....

....

Today's Date: **Last Night's Bedtime:**   **Wake Up Time:**

Name three good things about yesterday that you were grateful for last night:

....

....

....

Notes on how you feel/what you notice:

....

....

....

Today's Date: **Last Night's Bedtime:**   **Wake Up Time:**

Name three good things about yesterday that you were grateful for last night:

....

....

....

Notes on how you feel/what you notice:

....

....

....

INSPIRING STORIES OF INFINITE PURPOSE

A RESTED HEART BREEDS INSPIRED ART

"I'm living with the kind of ease that I didn't think was possible for me."

Those are the words of acclaimed visual artist Charlotte Schulz, who told us the shifts she experienced during *Infinite Purpose* are too numerous to count, from releasing anxieties to feeling divinely supported. But perhaps the greatest benefit of all has been all the good rest!

It's a small miracle, too. It has been decades, according to Charlotte, since she's felt so rested, so spiritually connected, and so at peace. As she read Spirit's missive on the importance of rest, she realized how much she'd been pushing herself, feeling drained and anxious.

"It's not that I don't have anxieties and difficulties anymore," she said. "It's just that I handle them differently and can move through them more quickly. I don't hang on to them as if it was my job to do so!"

Every night before bed, Charlotte now takes deep breaths and recalls the special and good things that happened that day. During the daytime, she has found her charcoal drawings have changed. Now that she's better rested and more at ease, she feels more open to a larger source for creative inspiration.

"I hadn't experienced a sense of being guided with making my art for a long time," she said. "Yet now, it is something I actively call forth and feel in complete cooperation with. I'm deeply grateful for the ways my life and work are transforming and growing."

You can view Charlotte's art online at charlotteschulz.com.

AWAKENING TO THE POWER OF YES

Two nights after poet and painter Julia Fehrenbacher began reading the *Infinite Purpose* teachings, she awakened in the middle of a deep sleep with a bold idea.

"I had been painfully stuck for weeks leading up to this aha," she said. "I wanted so very much to move forward with purpose and passion, toward that light-filled mission I knew I was here to carry out. I was frustrated, weighed down, and paralyzed with indecision. I was panicked and afraid I would be stuck in 'I don't knows' forever."

As she read Spirit's words, Julia felt the heaviness miraculously lifting. She still didn't know what was next, but her doubt was replaced with a deeply rooted knowing that it was all going to be okay and that an idea was on its way.

"I woke with a clarity of vision I've rarely experienced," she told us. At that point, Spirit hadn't even delivered the message on rest, which talks about divine inspiration striking during the sacred hours before dawn. But that's exactly what seemed to happen for Julia.

"There was a message for me, a very clear and specific message, that I must begin an online group called *The YES Movement*," Julia said. "And I must begin it right away, before all the details were worked out, before my mind had time to get in there and say *no*."

So, a couple days later Julia announced the group in a blog post with no plan in place and no major details revealed. To her delight, fifteen women said YES to walking into the wild unknown with her.

"I am now guiding myself and other women on the wild and beauty-filled path of living with love and purpose, to being all of whom we came here to be," Julia said. "I am awed by what happens when we allow the messages of Spirit to take us by the hand and lead us forward. Infinite, purposeful miracles happen. *Yes.* I'm so very thankful I said YES."

To meet Julia and learn about *The YES Movement*, go to paintedpath.org.

STEP FIVE

TUNING IN TO PROSPERITY

DURING THE FIRST HALF OF 1998, I SPENT A LOT OF TIME WITH OPRAH Winfrey. Well, sort of. The company I worked for had shut down, and I lost my dream job cohosting a national radio morning show for kids. Ashamed to be living off unemployment checks and receiving help from my parents, I turned on *Oprah* every day at four p.m. to help lift me out of my despair.

With no job leads and rapidly eroding confidence in my skills, I was getting daily headaches from crying so much. One afternoon, I wrote the following in my journal: "Today, Oprah said she thinks worrying and having faith are a contradiction in terms. She says anyone who believes in a higher power should trust that there is a plan, so there's no need to worry. But *I* think it's different when you have $300 million versus $60 to your name. I *do* believe God has a plan for me, but I'm worried it includes losing everything."

That day, I wrote out a prayer to God. "Please help me to see how wealthy I am despite what the bank statement says," I wrote. "Please help me find ways to be rewarded for my talents, and show me how to use them to better the Universe."

I'd love to tell you that little letter worked. But the truth is I didn't really want, or think I deserved, the kind of wealth I was asking for. I *was* gifted with all sorts of abundance, from being able to move in with my parents to having plenty of time to work on meaningful projects. But I was too focused on what I *lacked* to see what I *had*. Until my bank account was flush with money, I found it impossible to feel abundant.

I also felt sheepish about asking to be paid for using my talents to "better the Universe." I grew up with parents who worked in the nonprofit and education sectors, and it seemed to me that those who did good work in the world rarely got paid "good money" for it. Maybe it was greedy and pretentious, I thought, to think that I could achieve a vocational trifecta: get paid well, do what I love, *and* serve others. Who was *I* to ask for so much goodness?

I did find employment again, but that scarcity mindset—a sense I was never making or doing enough—haunted me for years. I read so many self-help books on attracting abundance, but I never felt like I got it right. When I worked in corporate communications, earning a great salary with benefits, I felt like I wasn't doing enough to help others. Once I left in 2007, hoping to use my gifts to be of service in the world, my income took an unexpected nosedive and we slipped into debt. I was right, I figured. I couldn't have it all. But then why did it seem some people *did*?

Lori and I bonded over this. She, too, struggled with deeply imbedded money issues for years. As we talked it through, we noticed the same thing was happening to each of us: when we were scared about where the next dollar was coming from, we felt distracted and unable to joyfully do our best work. Just scraping by wasn't doing us, or anyone else, any good. Lori even adopted a new mantra: *money serves my highest good.*

We both have done lots of work to cultivate an abundance mindset, but we felt transformed by Spirit's next teaching. In so many wise ways, it clarifies and offers healing for the power struggle with scarcity so many people face. We wish we'd had it years ago but trust this step has been revealed at the perfect time. We so hope that it feels equally rich to you. . . .

MESSAGE FROM SPIRIT

IN THIS MOMENT, INSIDE THE SECONDS OF THE MINUTES OF THE HOUR, you have everything you need. The things you say you cannot have are simply the result of the entrapments of your mind, of a lifetime of conditioning. You have been trained to believe you live in a state of lack. Even men with castles want *more* and will expend great amounts of energy and resources in pursuit of it: more money, more power, more accolades, more admiration, more companionship. And in their acts of desperation, rooted in a belief that there is not enough goodness for all, a pervasive emptiness often infiltrates their souls, regardless of how much *more* they have obtained.

The hyper-vigilant focus on personal lack within your circles of human interaction and influence is the ultimate distraction, routinely pulling you away from purpose and poisoning your relationship with joy. The act of longing is not an inviting-in, but a pushing-away, frequently and unintentionally creating the exact opposite of what it is you *think* you need. This has immediate implications for those engaged in the courageous answering of their divine calling.

Might we review the care instructions provided thus far? We have invited you into the wild unknown, where you are free to leave the burdens of human-made limitations behind. It is here that the floodgates to truth are opened and you can reveal the whole of your heart. Truthfulness instigates joyfulness, and they merge to reveal the path to purpose. You must be well rested for the journey in order to follow the guidance you receive.

Already, the shifts in you are palpable: hope rising up, meaning taking hold, new patterns forming, and clarity taking shape. But in the rearranging, in the dismantling of old walls, there is dust and debris tumbling through you, revealing old beliefs that sizzle like live wires, interrupting the flow of your electrical (vibrational) current. As this occurs, the light within you flickers, trying desperately to remain aglow.

This is the place at which you find yourself repeatedly, at the intersection of purposeful joy and mind-made distractions. So often, you have felt ready to fly, only to have your wings clipped by circumstance. At least this is the story you tell to yourself and others. The plot twists are frequently painted as hindrances, setbacks, and punishing blows to your soul's mission. It is easier to swallow the bitter pill of unfulfillment and explain your sense of stuckness if they are blamed on external factors, life circumstances that pulled you away from your path, whether losing your paper or losing your partner.

But what if, beloved, these unexpected earth-quakes, creating seismic shifts in your life, were invitations to deepen your connection to divinity, to experience the universe rearranging in deference to the Highest Good for all involved? When it feels as though your world is crumbling, like the very foundation beneath your feet is falling away, know that you are being led into the light of transformation.

We understand it is not comfortable, but growth is greatest in new seasons, when the spirit of you can no longer stand to exist just beneath the surface of life, like a seed about to sprout, and punches through to emerge anew. You gasp for air and shield your eyes, adjusting to the bright light of this new world, unsure how to exist without despair and disillusionment as your constant companions. All of Creation works to breathe blessings into your life in these moments of truth and transition, reminders that you are not alone nor helplessly lost. But you cannot feel held and guided by All of Creation when you run from it, insisting you know better, sure that you are protecting yourself by keeping your distance. How can you move forward, you ask, when you're feeling raw, vulnerable, and uncertain of what the future holds?

Carefully and consciously, we say. There is no better time to prepare yourself for abundance.

We hear you shouting, "Yes! I am ready! I am ready to attract abundance!"

And our reply, delivered with the utmost respect for your journey, is this: *No, beloved, you are not.*

In fact, you are ill prepared to receive the richness of life you long for but also run from. There was a time in your life when all of Goodness felt within reach and anything was possible. Maybe you were five, ten, fifteen, or twenty. You were closer to All That Is. You were closer to all you were meant to be.

You did not pay attention to the clock. If there was something you did not know, you said *I have time to learn it*. If there was something you saw that you wanted, you said *I have time to get it*. If there was something you wanted to try, you said *I have time to experience it*. If there was something you wanted to feel, you said *I'm going to feel it now*. Your *now* and your *future* were deeply entwined. You saw no separation. You delighted in the expectation that greatness was yours to create. You felt promise moving through your soul, pulsing through your body, and stirring in your mind.

There were voices early on that said, "You can be anything; what do you want to be?" The question was so big that you didn't know the answer. So you played with it. You tried on many hats. You instinctively helped people you cared about—with their shoelaces, with their lunch boxes, and with their hard feelings. You told many stories of who you were becoming. You were not naive, which the young

are often chided for. Rather, you were innately conscious and divinely connected, for you knew no other way to be.

As you experimented with your personality and gifts, you felt good when peers or adults smiled and clapped and bad when they didn't. Your ego was intrigued, and with its ever-growing and rather persuasive presence in the pit of your stomach, you learned to look outside yourself for validation. Whether you received praise or not, this is when the flow of abundance—the connection to your source of power—became frayed or blocked.

We invite you now to envision your life as a record album, playing the song of you. When the record was brand-new, upon your earthly arrival, the needle on the record player fit into every groove perfectly, and beautiful music emanated from it. You may not remember the tune of it, but you remember the feel of it. You danced and sang along at the top of your lungs, because it felt good and you knew your inner song by heart. *You were in the groove of Goodness from the moment you arrived on this spinning planet.*

The first time someone or something disrupted the rhythm of your song, intentional or not, the tiniest scratch appeared on your record, too small to impact your listening experience. But then it happened again, and the scratch expanded slightly. And then many times over, in ways you can't remember and others you can't forget. You kept singing and dancing, staying in the groove until the needle reached that scratch. You'd hear your record skip and feel your heart sink. With each passing year, and each new or deepening scratch, it became harder to listen to your own song.

Eventually, the needle could not ignore the ever-growing scratches, which had grown together, forming grooves of their own. The needle would get stuck there, repeating over and over the message of those blemishes on your record—"prepare to be disappointed; prepare to be hurt." The fear ingrained in those words spread from your head to your heart, and the scratches in your record seemed to multiply, changing the very rhythm of your song, of your earthly identity.

Have you ever heard two songs played at once? It is torturous for the mind, an assault on your senses, as you struggle to separate and make sense of the mismatched music and competing voices. This is why you may be feeling disoriented and depressed halfway through this journey. You were buoyed by the familiar strains of the song we are singing, the music you know by heart. But the more you listen and begin to find yourself inside its rhythm, the more that damaged record, full of scratches and skips that tell you all is not well, wants to be heard. *You* are not damaged, beloved. The record of your life *is*, with its lyrics changed from love and light to lack and loss. The solution is not to unplug the player or throw out the record, as Ego might suggest. This struggle is simply a case of misaligned grooves. *They are easier to repair than you think.*

If you research how to physically repair a scratch on a musical record, you will be advised to examine the scratch very closely with a magnifying tool, looking for dust and debris that have lodged inside the groove. Experts will tell you to first clear this with gentle care. They will then suggest a variety of tools, from needles to brushes, to slowly "lift" the scratch by following the original grooves it intersected. By carefully focusing and retracing the earliest lifelines of the record, the scratches can be, in effect, overridden.

This same approach, applied spiritually rather than physically, can repair the untruths that have become louder than the song of you, lifting the scratches, or elevating the vibration, that disrupted the harmonious partnership between you and the Glory of All (the record *and* the needle).

As we stated previously, the cultivation of joy is not for the faint of heart. It stirs hope and happiness in you but also exposes a deeply ingrained fear that experiencing joy again will only end in heart-break. What if you get engaged in work that fulfills and rewards you, only to lose it all? What if you heal from a hard relationship, only to land in another? What if you speak your truth and no one supports you in it? What if you rest well and miss something important?

Ah, but what if—by some miracle—what you consciously create is not ultimate-ly heartbreaking, but groundbreaking for you and others?

Note the depths of despair and disillusionment you have experienced in your lifetime, whether long ago or just now rising to the surface. It is easily all encompassing, yes? You hear yourself speaking of it, you feel it guiding your actions (or inaction), and your awareness of others' suffering some-how magnifies your own sense of dis-ease within yourself and in the world.

It is imperative that you *feel* your losses, honoring the emotions your body, mind, and spirit were meant to experience. To avoid them is to take a shortcut to stuckness. But to allow yourself to linger in them, to grow comfortable with discomfort and build a life around it, is to allow your brightest Self to get buried in the rubble, disconnected from your Source.

When you feel burdened by hardship or pained by circumstance, Joy feels like a villain. You resist it, find fault in it, and accuse it of taunting the weak ("how dare you be so happy when others are suffering!?"). Without proactively working to lift the scratches (or heal the deep wounds) and find your groove again, bereavement turns to bitterness, self-loathing replaces self-care, and your being in the world feels largely inconsequential.

Loss is a common thread that ties together all of humanity (alas, you are not alone in it!). It exists not to tear you apart, beloved, but to serve as a catalyst for positive change. To let grace lift the fog around you, slowly but surely, is to invite the Light back in. This is an act of courage and catapults you into living on purpose.

Herein lies the greatest advantage of opening yourself to the grief, the rage, and the worry that often comes with changes outside your control: You experience the powerful vibration of human emotion. It permeates throughout your life, ricocheting off the walls you've built around you, and you find yourself in what feels like an endless cycle of misfortune.

So imagine, beloved, the vibrational pull of *positive* emotions—of contentment, of relief, of excitement, and of trust—and their capacity to break down walls and lift you out into the glory of All That Is Possible! The energetic frequency of abundance is aligned with that of joy. They are a vibrational match, which allows them to exist in harmony and be fueled by one another. There are times in your life when you have experienced this perfect alignment, like finding two puzzle pieces that fit together. You felt elated and delighted by the synchronization of Goodness, and rightly so.

And yet abundance remains oddly elusive, yes? You ask for it, you envision it coming to you, and sometimes it does (oh joy!). But sometimes it doesn't appear as you'd hoped, or it seems to disappear just as quickly as it came. This is evidence that there is misalignment in the vibrational frequency of your emotions and your visions of abundance. The wounds you have experienced in your life, like scratches to your record, may have been partially healed but are holding debris that disrupts conscious creation.

Please observe the woman in Lori's painting (on page 92). Notice everything about her that stands out to you: the way she is dressed, the view from where she is sitting, the flowers in her hair, the relaxed state of being she is in, or her poised stature. Notice the aspects of this image that seem particularly attractive to you and the assumptions you make about her. This image of a woman at peace—comfortable in her own skin, creatively adorned in bright colors and patterns, with time

to savor her beautiful surroundings and the means to place her in such a setting—can serve as inspiration or send you into a downward spiral of desperation, wishing and wanting rather than creating the same for yourself. Be honest today in your reaction to her. Notice the emotions that rise to your surface. What about her do you see in yourself and vice versa?

We will tell you the secret of her inner peace: she is gently focused on joy *and* abundance not only in this moment, but in all moments. In every second of every minute of every hour, she believes wholeheartedly that she has everything she needs and expects that more is miraculously on its way. She trusts not only that she has enough, but that she is enough: worth every penny, every opportunity, every breath of fresh air, every restful night, every bite of good food, every act of kindness, every rich friendship, and every invitation into deeper joy. In this state of being, she not only attracts light, but radiates it.

Again, pay close attention to your reactions to this news. Does your mind shift to jealousy or doubt, to feeling "less than" because you have not reached this state of enlightened abundance or abundant enlightenment? Or do you see her as an invitation, as evidence that the same is possible for you? (Take heart. It is.)

We encourage you today to envision one kind of abundance flowing into your life, the kind you most often daydream about or long for. Many of you will imagine various iterations of financial security, others will long for plenty of time to reflect and create, while still others will envision experiencing loving and evolving relationships. There is no right answer beyond choosing the one that you suspect you need most to feel secure, to consistently experience true joy.

Within your vision of this, you will have to create your own measuring stick. Abundance is a weighted word in your culture; it is unquantifiable and nearly undefinable. One person's *more* is not enough for another.

So, envision first for yourself what just enough would feel like—enough to feel secure, enough to feel supported, and enough to feel grateful. Now, ask yourself honestly if this sense of enough also triggers fears of lack in you—doubts of it lasting, worries about someday needing more, or judgment of others who do have more. You can feel joy waning and tension rising. If this rubble exists, know that the debris of lack is still tumbling through you and throwing off your vibration.

If you don't see it appearing yet, then please continue your envisioning and imagine having not just enough, but *more* than enough. What does this look like to you? How does it feel? If there are negative emotions threatening the positive ones, tell them you see them: the doubt that this kind of abundance is possible, the concerns about having too much when others have too little, the sense you're not worthy or that you haven't rightly earned this much goodness. Know it, feel it, and name it. There is healing power even in the shift from skipping over the scratches to examining them closely.

In the coming days, we ask that you notice where and when this sense of lack emerges for you. You shall be a conscious observer of your own actions in your two-step with abundance. Where do you get tripped up? What is the message that keeps playing in your head, interrupting your song? We encourage you to write down what you see and say the following as you do:

"I RELEASE YOU TODAY, AS I JOYFULLY SHIFT INTO A CONSTANT STATE OF ENERGETIC ALIGNMENT WITH GOODNESS."

This is the critical work of preparing yourself for abundance. You shall feel us by your side, assisting in releasing the toxins of unworthiness, the fears of insecurity, and the talons of scarcity that have dug deep into your being. It may feel as though you're humming a new tune, but in truth, you're simply remembering the song of you. It is our favorite sound.

REFLECTION FIVE

CHANGE YOUR TUNE

IN STEP FIVE, SPIRIT ENCOURAGES YOU TO NOTICE WHEN "A SENSE OF LACK EMERGES IN YOU" AND USE EACH INSTANCE AS AN OPPORTUNITY TO REFRAME YOUR PERSPECTIVE AND, IN ESSENCE, REWRITE YOUR SONG.

As you move through your days, here are some scarcity triggers to be on the lookout for: the reactions you have to someone who seems to have more money than you; your self-talk as you're making a purchase; how you compare yourself to neighbors, friends, or colleagues; how you feel when others ask what you do; and the moments you catch yourself longing for something (from a new car to a romantic relationship).

Use these pages to write down when these or similar moments occur and the limiting belief that immediately pops up. You might begin to notice some common themes. After each moment you write about, write or recite the following sentence (a new mantra to replace the beliefs that no longer serve you):

"I RELEASE YOU TODAY, AS I JOYFULLY SHIFT INTO A CONSTANT STATE OF ENERGETIC ALIGNMENT WITH GOODNESS."

WHAT HAPPENED?
Write down what happened that triggered insecurity and scarcity in you.

....
....
....

HOW DID YOU REACT?
Write out the limiting belief that you immediately said to yourself.

....
....
....

RELEASE IT
"I release you today, as I joyfully shift into a constant state of energetic alignment with Goodness.

....
....
....

WHAT HAPPENED?
Write down what happened that triggered insecurity and scarcity in you.

HOW DID YOU REACT?
Write out the limiting belief that you immediately said to yourself.

RELEASE IT
"I release you today, as I joyfully shift into a constant state of energetic alignment with Goodness.

WHAT HAPPENED?
Write down what happened that triggered insecurity and scarcity in you.

HOW DID YOU REACT?
Write out the limiting belief that you immediately said to yourself.

RELEASE IT
"I release you today, as I joyfully shift into a constant state of energetic alignment with Goodness.

WHAT HAPPENED?
Write down what happened that triggered insecurity and scarcity in you.

....

....

....

HOW DID YOU REACT?
Write out the limiting belief that you immediately said to yourself.

....

....

....

RELEASE IT
"I release you today, as I joyfully shift into a constant state of energetic alignment with Goodness.

....

....

....

Note: A wallet-sized printable abundance mantra is available online at **yourinfinitepurpose.com/resources** *with the password* **MAGICMAKERS**.

INSPIRING STORIES OF INFINITE PURPOSE

HEALING FROM THE GROUND UP

When Christy Marek graduated from college with a degree in Child Psychology, she felt drawn to work with children suffering from life-limiting or terminal illnesses. But she was scared that kind of work would be emotionally draining and often heartbreaking. So she pushed that dream aside for twenty years, ignoring every sign and related opportunity that came into view.

Finally, the nudges grew too strong to ignore. Christy worked with a therapist to release her fears. And she felt divinely guided to start meditating outdoors for twenty minutes every day, rain or shine—or snow! That daily ritual of lying down upon the earth and connecting with its energies was as healing as she'd hoped.

When Christy heard about *Infinite Purpose*, she was ready to move forward and eager to be divinely inspired on her path. Christy was deeply impacted by the messages from Spirit, but it was Step Five with Lori's painting of a woman meditating outside that brought her to tears.

"Here, without having known how or why, was a painting of me, of the spirit of how I feel each and every day communing with nature and connecting with my deepest purpose," she said. And when she read the words on the painting, *"Prepare Yourself for Abundance,"* they seemed miraculously meant for her, too. That's exactly what she'd been doing in her meditation project, she told us—preparing for the abundance of goodness that could come from stepping into her calling.

Within months, Christy was doing the courageous work she'd avoided for years. "These kids are changing my life for the better," she said. "I am growing, moving further off the beaten path, and loving every invigorating minute of it!"

For more information on Christy and her work, go to wonderofallthings.com.

TRADING BUSYNESS FOR HAPPINESS

Writer Angie Mizzell wasn't sure why she felt drawn to read *Infinite Purpose*, but she didn't question the pull. As she dove in, each message felt like balm for the soul.

"Some were reminders of universal truths I've learned on my own journey," she told us. "And others helped me dissolve the resistance that remained, particularly where rest and joy were concerned."

But it was this fifth message, on preparing for abundance, which rocked Angie's world.

"My jaw dropped. It felt like a message written for me," she said. "The language about the record player, the singing, dancing, and clapping . . . the time when everything began to change . . . the loss. It felt like I was reading a key turning point scene in my memoir-in-progress."

Angie felt like it was a divine reminder that her work is important and to be patient with its unfolding. She told us it took months to fully process this truth. First, she said, she had to actually decide to make following her purpose a priority. Then, she began to sort out her commitments and release some things that kept her busy, but not fulfilled.

"I'm always taking on too much, and I know that it's all based on fear— fear that if I stop 'doing,' I'll become irrelevant," she said. "I now understand that my path to abundance is not paved with stress and fatigue."

Today, she's taking inspired action, grateful for what she calls an "amazing journey" that carried her deeper into her calling. Learn more about Angie at angiemizzell.com.

STEP SIX

HOW PURPOSE IS BORN

WHEN LORI READ THIS NEXT TEACHING, SHE WAS SPEECHLESS. SPIRIT'S detailed description of her painting erased any previous doubts she'd had about their working through her, guiding her creative process. You might recall that Spirit first approached me about *Infinite Purpose* on the day Lori learned that eight of her paintings had been "rejected" by the publisher she was working with on a big project. She'd created dozens of pieces of art for them, each one a little reflection of her heart, and she felt so deflated when they said these particular paintings didn't work for them. Spirit swooped in right away, letting me know those eight paintings were not meant for that project, but had been "commissioned" for a new collaboration.

Naturally, Lori was both amazed *and* skeptical. She thought those paintings were perfect for the project she was working on, not destined for something else. But as each message from Spirit came through, mentioning specific details about the art chosen to accompany it, she realized something bigger had been at work and remembered how certain she had felt about the composition of these particular paintings.

For instance, when Lori first painted the artwork Spirit chose to illustrate this next teaching, there was a field with just one sunflower. But as she looked at it, Lori just *knew* it needed to become a field full of sunflowers. She made that change, but the painting still didn't feel finished. She asked her angels for help, and soon Lori knew her next step: she needed to add a cardinal on the left. Once she did this, she sent the painting to the publisher.

"But I couldn't stop thinking about that scene," she says. "The bird was looking out in the distance, like he was waiting for something. I could tell something was missing." Once again, Lori sat back down at her art table and waited again for inspiration to strike.

"I waited until I clearly knew what it needed: a sec-

ond cardinal," she recalls. "I knew there were supposed to be two birds in the painting, together.
Honestly, when I think back on that moment,
I felt hope. I felt back in creative alignment,
like I was co-creating the artwork with some
creative force out there. The painting finally
felt right."

But when Lori turned the new version into
the publishing company, her contacts responded
with disappointment. They thought both birds were dis-
tracting and opted not to use the painting at all. Lori felt confused
and deflated because she'd been so clear during the process of creating that artwork, inspired to make the changes she did. The publisher's rejection made her
question what she'd felt and doubt her abilities.

Only when she read this next teaching were her creative instincts validated.
Lori called me, totally awestruck after reading this line from Spirit: "Where there
was one bird, there are now two; where there was one sunflower, there now are
many."

"That was the exact process I went through in creating this painting," she told
me. "I love knowing that Spirit really, truly was guiding me! It's so amazing."

As you dive into this next step of the journey, we hope you see the power of
honoring *your* connection to the Great Beyond, moving forward when inspiration
strikes. It's your time to fly. . . .

You are here
to harvest hope

MESSAGE FROM SPIRIT

WE WISH TO SPEAK WITH YOU NOW ABOUT WHAT YOU SEE VERSUS who you are.

When you look in the mirror, you do not see a true representation of you. You see the opposite, and yet you keep looking and accepting it as truth. The mirror does not provide you with an accurate reflection of how others see you, either, for they can only see you through their own eyes, their own altered perspectives. Sometimes this viewpoint is as backwards as what you see in the mirror. Pay no mind to false reflections. They deteriorate the fabric of you, fraying the edges until you come unraveled.

Only the Light Eternal can see you accurately, for you were made in its image. You are part of the electromagnetic spectrum of light that ripples and radiates through the universe, and your eyes are only capable of processing a fraction of this light.

Your appearance has very little to do with your ability to live on purpose, but your self-reflection has everything to do with it.

You say, *I am ugly.* We see only beauty.

You say, *I am broken.* We see you as whole.

You say, *I need more.* We see all is well.

You say, *I am unloved.* We see you as loved unequivocally.

You say, *I don't know what to do next.* We say you are here to harvest hope. Start there.

In a state of lack, you have double vision. You look into the mirror and see what you hear: the scarcity in your mind, the voices in your head, and the voices outside of your Self, all reporting the opposite of who you really are. But there is an inkling, the tiniest glimmer of awareness, of a second vision of you, isn't there? It is OUR vision of you: beautiful, whole, abundant, and perfect. A beacon of hope for yourself and the world around you.

When you were a baby, you loved to look at your reflection because you saw what we see. You weren't afraid to marvel at yourself, to be awed by the light beaming back at you. This is the being of light you came here to be!—*the true reflection of you*—and we wish for you to embrace this today.

Let us speak first of the notion of planets aligning. In this common saying, you indicate an occurrence of divine synchronicity. People who dwell in the fields of astronomy and physics may argue that planetary alignment is impossible. More-over, their data suggests that, were the seven scientifically recognized planets in your solar system to perfectly align with the earth and with each other, it would have no felt impact—gravitationally *or* spiritually. We applaud the exploration of this area that you define as space but respectfully encourage you to recognize the vastness and purposefulness of the universe in which these planets exist.

To have a sense of where your planet, your physical home base, fits within this line-up provides emotional comfort. You feel tethered within a methodically designed "solar system" (meaning that you and the planets revolve around light), surely made for a reason. There is a vibrational exchange between one planet and the next, and to the ether around it all, that presents itself like a beautifully cho-reographed dance. Some will explain it as coincidence or luck, the way these plan-ets coexist, and even assert that all are not necessary for the universe to thrive.

In fact, the more sophisticated the instruments, the more unsettled some become with the discovery of matter and small-but-mighty planets that exist in the in-between and others that exist beyond comprehension. There is no scientific explanation for them. To investigate them all would be a daunting and unending task for human beings. And so, you are left with mystery. These planets, galaxies, and force fields spin on, widely ignored, even categorized as "minor" despite their incredible girth. Rest assured, every speck of matter fulfills a purpose in the universe. That you cannot explain it all is a gift in itself.

What you know "for certain" about space, and what you know of its purpose, is a reflection of what you have been told. The same is true for your existence within it.

We wish to tell you your birth story. Not the one you have heard or reconstructed of your physical arrival on the earth, but the story of what took place just before your journey to humanity. You will find no scientific explanation for it, but perhaps it will give definition to your faith in infinite purpose.

The highs and lows of your human experience, from elation to devastation, are meeting the expectations of your soul's stated desires. Perhaps this seems preposterous to you. Why would you have signed up for the life you've lived? It is important that you know your soul felt absolutely capable of and excited for this mission.

Liv, we are placing an image in your mind. Could you please describe what you see?

LIV: *Okay, yes. I've actually seen this image flash before me all week and wasn't sure what it meant. I'm seeing dozens or maybe hundreds of beings—like bodies made of light—standing in rows that just go on and on, and they're all facing the same direction. Kind of like an army receiving commands. It seems really dark in the distance, and actually all around them, but there are twinkling stars, too. It's like they're standing on a giant platform in the middle of space, but their bodies are so bright that there's plenty of light to see.*

SPIRIT: *And how would you describe their demeanor and*

appearance?

LIV: *Well, I can't see their faces and they're all standing still, so I can't read their body language. But they seem very calm, very focused on whatever they're looking at or listening to. They're all the same height, probably the same weight, there's nothing to distinguish one from another.*

SPIRIT: *Take a closer look. We are magnifying the appearance of one light being. Please describe in detail what you see.*

LIV: *Oh! Oh, my gosh. I was thinking it was just overall fuzzy light. But now I can see that this "body" is made of probably millions of grid lines that look like the most delicate threads and they glow! It's like graph paper made of light, but the lines sometimes crisscross and there's this sparkle, like a tiny light bulb, wherever the lines meet. And I can see colors, too! Like tiny colored dots, zipping so fast up and down these threads that they're like streaks of color. It's like a whole transit system of light and movement. And then there are these colors—wow—that are just radiating through the center of this body, like from head to toe. I guess it's kind of like the chakras that I know, but it looks more like a stream or column of rainbow-colored lines moving up and down. I'm trying to come up with a way to explain it, but I've never seen anything like it. Instead of all separate chakras, like balls of specific colors spinning, it's like they've blended together in bands of light.*

SPIRIT: *This is a sufficient explanation. We thank you. You have just seen the soul.*

A body of light, indeed, so intricately illuminated that it defies human logic. You have witnessed a battalion of souls receiving guidance for their earthly missions, for which they are serenely and supremely excited. They are aware of and fascinated by the emotional terrain, eager to experience the high highs and low lows, which they perceive to all be intensely beautiful expressions of love or curious tantrums of the ego. They have been told of the complexities of human emotions and situational circumstances and the challenges associated with allowing the light of their souls to illuminate what is possible, while the shadows of their minds would attempt the opposite.

And now we shall shift our language, dear reader, to allow you to see that the *they* we speak of is also the *you* we are speaking to. Indeed, you not only agreed to this earthly life, but had a hand in creating it, selecting—from an array of possibilities presented by the benevolent universe—the circumstances into which you could be born, soulfully aware of the steps required to use this life for Good.

We now return to the vision provided to and described by Liv of that battalion of souls-in-agreement and in-alignment, which you have experienced but understandably forgotten. This commitment ceremony is conducted to imprint the Truth of All on your soul so that you know who you are when what's not needed falls away, and so when you are provided opportunities to spread light, you feel a stirring in your soul . . . like hearing a song you knew long ago.

Please prepare yourself to experience the truth of who you are. Breathe deeply, beloved, as you receive what we are about to share.

We will now reveal portions of your exchange with the Powers That Be, a celebration and confirmation of your Divine Self, made in advance of your earthly incarnation. We invite you to audibly recite the questions you were asked and the answers you provided, to feel the full vibrational pull of them. You may experience a slight memory of them, or an innate connection to them. Like gravity suspending planets, we raise you up within the echoes of your words.

Are you ready for a mission of such high order?

I am.

Are you prepared to spend an extended period of time in isolation and incubation as you grow acclimated to the rhythmic and vibrational differences between here and Earth?

I am.

Are you aware that you shall be thrust into a world of emotional extremes, potentially adversarial to your sensitive ways?

I am.

Are you willing to work your entire life to quiet the voices of Ego and see grace in the face of pain in order to radiate the innate light of your being?

I am.

Are you dedicated to recognizing joy as a guide?

I am.

Are you consciously committed to returning Home feeling fulfilled rather than flummoxed by your experiences?

I am.

Are you aware that much of this agreement will be buried by external voices and that part of your mission—potentially strenuous but eternally helpful—is to uncover it within you?

I am.

Are you also dedicated to finding and honoring the gifts given to you for this journey—traits, talents, passions, intuitions—as tools for experiencing joy?

I am.

When you come across wayward souls, those who have been unwittingly silenced by the strains of their experience, are you willing to use these gifts to offer them light?

I am.

Are you willing to return Home when called, whether because your mission is complete, the light of your being is needed elsewhere, or because the absence of it on Earth has potential to serve as a catalyst for positive change in human beings you influenced and inspired?

I am.

Are you open to receiving communication and guidance from the Powers That Be and celestial beings who address only your highest good via physical signals, ethereal voices, sacred readings, earthly teachers, and nature's blessings?

I am.

Are you aware that you are loved beyond measure?

I am.

Then you are ready, beloved.

We would ask, before we continue, that you breathe again. Let the breadth of this celebration of your Divine Self move through you, find itself in you. Yes, there.

Souls, including yours, that are granted the gift of earthly life are fascinated by and eager to experience the emotional terrain of humanity. You were keenly aware of the unique set of circumstances provided to human beings, allowing for a full spectrum of emotional highs and lows. Though hard for your mind to comprehend, your soul delighted in the invitation to feel the full spectrum of light and dark in this life, every color and every feeling, intent on using each experience as a brightening of its own light. Before you arrived here, your soul was already looking forward to reporting back on all it would experience in this life.

To your soul, this appears to be a game of playful and passionate pursuit, focused on finding and cultivating joy. But as you have experienced, such a task is markedly complicated by your mind and body, which have not been equally informed or engaged in this mission. They are caught up in the daily minutia of earthly life while your soul seeks opportunities to pursue its higher purpose. That you now see the misalignment of this makes space for you to adjust and honor that which your soul came to accomplish.

Your soul has one desired outcome of this earthly life—to radiate joy—and you must determine the best courses of (inspired!) action in order to do this consistently. You are, in essence, a missionary sent to help shift the vibrational frequency of your planet so that it is energetically aligned with Goodness. Your soul approached this with playfulness and delight, not angst or a sense of being burdened.

So, before you question how on earth you are supposed to fulfill such a mission when your mind and heart feel inconsistently joyful, please turn your attention to the painting by Lori that coincides with this teaching (see page 112).

When it feels as though all is lost, please do not lose hope. It is what brought you here, beloved. Sow the seeds of it, take good care of it, celebrate the growth of it, and share your bounty with others. Remember that when you look into a mirror, you do not see your true reflection, but a mirage of opposites and untruths. When you allow yourself to see only what *we* see, the truest and purest reflection of the light being that is you, all of Goodness in your midst multiplies.

Where there was once one bird, there are now two. Where there once was one sunflower, there now are many. That is because this is where hope is born, in the unending fields of possibility you committed to planting and cultivating. Hope is an expectation of Good to come, felt as a fluttering in your heart and an unwinding of the tightrope that has been wrapped around your spirit.

Hope is how light reaches people who have lost their way, the wayward souls you committed to helping by leveraging the gifts you were given. Remember? When you harvest hope for another soul, you feel the light in you, the purpose of you, begin to expand. And slowly, you begin to see your own Self-reflection—that of a glorious being of light who is here on purpose and is deeply loved. You are, you are, you are.

REFLECTION SIX

GROWING HOPE

The Hdy

SPIRIT USES THIS TEACHING TO PUT THE POWER OF HOPE FRONT AND CENTER, REMINDING US OF OUR SOULS' COMMITMENT TO CULTIVATE IT—FOR OURSELVES AND FOR OTHERS—IN THIS EARTHLY LIFE: "SOW THE SEEDS OF IT, TAKE GOOD CARE OF IT, CELEBRATE THE GROWTH OF IT, AND SHARE YOUR BOUNTY WITH OTHERS." MOST OF US HAVE NEVER LOOKED AT HOPE IN THIS WAY, AS SOMETHING TO BE SO CAREFULLY TENDED TO. THESE PAGES ARE MEANT TO OPEN YOUR EYES TO HOW YOU'RE ALREADY ACHIEVING THIS AND HOW YOU WANT IT TO EXPAND.

How have you sowed the seeds of hope? Each planting season, gardeners sow their seeds by placing them in prepared soil and making sure they are protected beneath the surface, giving them the best chance to thrive. How have you planted the seeds of hope in your life, and what conditions have been necessary to let them take root and grow? Some possibilities might include intentionally looking for encouraging friends, choosing to look on the bright side of a hard situation, working your way into an inspiring or faith-based circle or organization, or reading and watching materials that lift you up. Share here what gives you hope and how you've incorporated that into your life.

How have you taken good care of those seeds of hope you've planted? No expert gardener would just leave the seeds she's planted and expect them to grow with gusto. She'll add water and fertilizer, which provides essential nutrients that the soil doesn't provide on its own. So, consider the conscious choices *you've* made to ensure that hope takes root and continues to grow. Maybe you've nurtured certain relationships, limited your exposure to negativity, practiced what you've learned from others, or made bold choices that have supercharged your growth. Make note of them here.

....

....

....

....

....

....

How do you celebrate hope's growth in your life? We love that Spirit is encouraging us all not to just plow through, but to periodically pause to honor the ways hope has given us wings. When have *you* celebrated hope? Maybe you've delighted in achieving a goal, rewarded yourself for moving through something difficult, affirmed yourself in the mirror, or paused to soak in the positive changes in your life. Write down what you're celebrating.

....

....

....

....

How have you shared your bounty with others? Have you ever received a handpicked bouquet of gorgeous blooms from a friend who grew them herself? It is the sweetest gift and a guaranteed day brightener. So, too, is receiving guidance and support from someone who consciously, carefully cultivates hope. If you have given hope to someone else, you know the miracle that happens. You're not left with less for yourself, but instead hope multiplies, lifting *you* up as you lift someone else up. When have you experienced this? Whom have you encouraged, supported, or guided with hope?

....

....

....

....

....

....

As you've reflected on the ways you've cultivated hope, what has been stirred within you? Are you feeling inspired to do more? To try something different? To deepen your daily relationship with hope? Share what's come to the surface.

....

....

....

....

....

....

INSPIRING STORIES OF INFINITE PURPOSE

CHANGING THE WAY WE SEE AUTISM

As the mom of a child on the autism spectrum, Tera Girardin knows firsthand how overwhelming an autism diagnosis can be for parents. But whenever she'd take her son to his therapy center, her spirits were lifted as she witnessed her son and other children with ASD (autism spectrum disorder) making amazing progress.

"I wanted to tell people about all the small victories and the delightful spirits of those children," Tera said.

So, Tera leveraged her skills as a portrait photographer to create local fundraisers that have given families hope and made their kids feel like superstars, including a wall calendar featuring their photos. She felt good about each endeavor, but it seemed something was missing.

One day in the car, Tera was contemplating the *Infinite Purpose* teaching she'd read earlier in the day and wondered if Spirit would help her realize what she needed to do next. Right then, Tera says she had a "light-bulb moment." A clear, divine whisper told her to create a book—one that not only features gorgeous photos of kids with ASD, but enchanting stories about them and inspiring insights from their parents. A new way to harvest hope.

"It was something that I suddenly just felt at my core. I *knew* it was a calling," Tera said. "It was exciting and scary, but I didn't raise doubts or dwell on how I was going to do it. I just enjoyed the excitement of *knowing*."

Still driving, Tera realized her exit was ahead. Her attention shifted to the car directly in front of her. The license plate said MAGICAL. Tera squealed with delight; it felt like a playful sign from the universe that she was on the right path. Energized and excited, Tera began scheduling photo shoots for her new project, *Faces of Autism, Stories of Hope*, and people came out of the woodwork to help, from offering to design a logo to providing publishing expertise. Magical, indeed! For updates on the book, go to teraphotography.com.

LIFE SUPPORT FOR WOMEN IN TRANSITION

As a Registered Respiratory Therapist, Kim Flatland has spent decades helping people breathe. But after a difficult divorce in 2006, it felt like *she* was gasping for air. Kim did everything she could to heal her heart and soul, from tapping into her intuition to employing the power of affirmations. At one point, she even had a self-help book in the works, but she let it go due to creative differences with the publisher. Kim struggled to figure out what more she was meant to do with her life—until *Infinite Purpose* came along.

"There has been a sense of calm within my soul like never before," she said. "Everything I'd studied and believed finally made its way to the deepest part of me. My ego finally stopped fighting it, and I had clear instructions for living it."

Kim was especially struck by Step Six and repeatedly recited the *"I AM"* mantras Spirit provided. For her, it was reminiscent of the holy words repeated at a baptismal service. She could feel transformation taking place. Kim sensed that she was ready to harvest and share all that she had learned in her "growing season." She asked the universe to show her a sign that this was the case.

A few days later, Kim received an automated email sent from a file upload system where, years before, her book editor had asked that she send her manuscript. After the deal fell through and Kim's computer died, she'd long figured the files were gone. But this surprise email said that, due to inactivity on her account, she now needed to take action and download the files.

Kim could hardly believe that her words of hope, inspired by her own healing journey, had returned to her. She *was* ready to take action. Within a few months, she launched loveyoursoulself.com, with resources and personal reflections, including the writings originally intended for her book, to help women move through life transitions feeling confident and connected.

STEP SEVEN

FROM LOST TO FOUND

BACK WHEN SPIRIT TOLD ME TO PHOTOGRAPH AND WRITE ABOUT everyday beauty, 365 days in a row, it was so incredibly healing that I continued the practice for a second year. But eventually, I began to feel a little lost at sea.

The blog still resonated with many readers, but it wasn't bringing in any income—or personal fulfillment. So I spent most of my days not really doing what I *loved*, but what I was pretty good at—copywriting and consulting for big brands, with a little blogging and beauty spotting on the side. I had a new baby, too, whose special needs became increasingly apparent as he reached toddlerhood. I shared none of this with readers, though. They came to my blog for beauty, I told myself—not to hear about my struggles.

I posted less and less, and my readership began to dwindle (and, with that, invitations to speak or write about the power of everyday beauty faded away). The economy tanked, and my income shrank as copywriting clients disappeared and budgets tightened at the radio station where I cohosted a weekly show on living your best life. It was so scary to sink into deep debt. With nearly constant calls from creditors, I didn't even want to be in my own home.

I was willing to try anything to help keep our family afloat—even telling the truth. One day, I ran across an article about the power of vulnerability in blogging. The writer asked the following question: "Who are you, *really*, and how do you show that to your readers?" Those were scary questions for me. I had always been very cautious about keeping my posts as impersonal and generic as possible, hoping to please everyone and avoid conflict or ridicule. And I *rarely* shared anything that was spiritual in nature, even though I was increasingly aware of and wowed by angels and spirits in my midst.

For instance, when an angel appeared in a photo I'd taken of melting ice outside my front door, I wrote about it very nonchalantly, asking if anyone else could see her outline. But the truth was that I was *flipping out*. I knew she was a sign, a messenger of hope at my doorstep, and I was floored by every tiny, angelic detail in that ice sculpture no bigger than my thumb.

I didn't share stories like that because I worried people wouldn't like me, wouldn't hire me, and wouldn't take me seriously. But that strategy clearly wasn't working. Inspired by the question of how I was showing my readers the *real* me, I took a risk and posted fifteen true facts about myself on the blog.

"It's harder than it sounds, deciphering the things that are really and truly part of my spirit versus the things I've learned, changed, or hidden about myself just to fit in," I wrote. Most of the personal truths I shared were pretty mundane, but I peppered in several jaw-droppers: "When I was little, I used to sing to angels and spirits in my backyard." To my surprise, my inbox was flush with kind comments, thank you notes, and requests for *more* personal insights. I was so relieved and so touched by the response, my heart nearly burst.

One of those comments read, "You are beautiful and wise, and I love all of these things about you!" It came from an artist named Lori Portka.

Lori and I had already exchanged a few emails, having admired each other's work online, and I was so happy that she not only still liked me, but maybe even liked me more for telling the truth. She became a cheerleader for me as I shared more and more of my authentic self online, quickly gaining new readers, seizing new opportunities, and opening up to my intuitive gifts. She claims I inspired her to do the same. Instead of hiding behind her paintings, she began telling the real and raw life stories that inspired them.

Long before we knew we'd be working on *Infinite Purpose* together, we had a heart-to-heart about the depth of our friendship. We had this deep sense that our souls came into this life on a mission to find each other. "You feel like *home* to me," I told her.

So when this next message came through from Spirit, it brought us to tears—because we know the magic of being truthful about and loved for who we are and why we're here. And we want the same for you.

MESSAGE FROM SPIRIT

YOU ARE NOT RACING TOWARD A FINISH LINE. FULFILLMENT IS NOT A final destination. A racing heart is not an indication of contentment. And yet you often seem preoccupied with getting everything done "on time" or citing age or circumstance as reasons for rushing into plans, hastily preparing for future projects and cautiously imagining your ideal outcomes. You have specific parameters for success: how many, how much, how often, how well. You compare yourself and your journey to others', collecting evidence for the case you've long built against yourself—the Ego-driven scolding that rains down on you, even (or especially) after a string of light-filled days. It would have you believe that too much of a good thing is a bad thing. In truth, there is no such thing as too much good.

When you allow yourself to believe that there is not enough good, you feel longing at the core of you, a fuzzy fog of homesickness intruding on the light around your heart. It was not your soul's intent, nor that of All That Is Good, for you to spend your earthly life longing for Home. And yet, you have known the misery of feeling lost, alone, unseen, unheard, unlike the others, or unsure of the future. When left to fester, this fear can grow debilitating, cutting you off from your Source.

Some seek to self-regulate, managing this misery by forcibly silencing it. There are temporary escapes that feed the Ego—growing bitter, misplacing anger, belittling others, finding fault, running away, or inviting in chaos—but these do not satisfy the soul. These knee-jerk reactions to soul-deep longing become salt in the wounds they attempted to hide.

Repeated employment of these escape strategies, or undermining the wisdom of your Divine Self by choosing an altered (and artificial) state of being, only contributes to a sense of mistaken identity, of being an outsider in your own life.

Rather than perseverate on your sense of homesickness, we ask instead that you actively make yourself at home. Before you came, you did not agree to live like an outsider looking in, but to assimilate in order to experience the divinely orchestrated nature of being human.

It is the only way to continuously experience the serendipitous and euphoric merging of your spiritual life with your earthly life, not separate, but coexisting and co-creating as One. Those who subconsciously opt to avoid or ignore their soul agreement shall not experience the bliss of a wholly integrated existence, while the same fate is destined for those who claim to be so spiritually sound that their earthly responsibilities are avoided, ignored, or feared.

You are holy, beloved, and wholly capable of deriving pure joy from the flow of consciousness and creativity that exists in an awakened state. It is what we are here to teach so that each and every one of you finds your Self divinely inspired, with clear instructions on how to move forward.

So, let us speak first of moving forward. Rare is the human being who has not been required or invited to move their belongings to another home, another neighborhood, another city, another country, or to another side of the planet. You are not in the very same place you have always been, correct? If you were, this would signal stifled growth, for expansion both requires and creates movement.

Consider the last time you moved from one space to another. Depending on the circumstances, you experienced delight or dread: delight over the place and the new possibilities it represented, or dread over what you were leaving behind and a foreboding uncertainty about the future. Faith and fear meet again! Either way, your instinct was to make your new arrangements as comfortable as possible, whether you had a corner of a room or plenty of room to roam. You knew what it would take to make your new space feel like home.

We ask now that you work with us to create your own comfort zone—not physically, but with the power of your mind. When the momentum of positive thought is paired with your soul's intentions to address a common goal, the results can feel phenomenal.

Note: *What follows is a guided meditation provided by Spirit. You can read through the content or listen to an audio version online at yourinfinitepurpose.com/resources (password is MAGICMAKERS). There is space on pages 141 and 142 to write down your experience.*

We invite you to create the comforts of home within you, not just around you. Please visualize yourself walking down a winding road, so beautiful and serene that it stirs your soul. You don't know where you are; you don't need to. You need only know it is your own Nirvana. Notice the colors around you. Notice the sounds you hear. Feel a slight breeze touch your cheek and tousle your hair. All is well.

Now notice a pathway to your right, an offshoot of this road that you know you must follow. You have no fear of trespassing, of bumping into a stranger, or of finding something unwanted at the end of the path. Release any such fears in order to remain in alignment with Goodness, led by grace.

When you step onto this pathway made for you, a deep calm washes over you. The burdens of your earthly life fall away, and you feel wholly present, even excited, for whatever comes next. You can sense this path leads only to some place Good. There is a gate ahead of you, beautiful and inviting, that must lead to this Good place. As you reach it, you take a deep, centering breath. You are buzzing with excited anticipation.

You push open the gate. A little nudge is all it takes for it to open wide, and you gasp at the beauty of what you see: the most beautiful, perfect home you could imagine. Take in the details that speak to you. Notice what surrounds it. Do you see water? Woods? Mountains? Sky?

As you approach this dream home of yours, the front door opens and someone emerges, waving wildly and happily to you and then motioning you to come forward, clearly delighted that you've arrived. You feel so loved, so cared for, so celebrated! You receive the warmest embrace as you approach, and you're led inside. You are warmly embraced by another dear soul who adores you. Whether or not you recognize them doesn't matter. Simply linger there for a moment to receive—fully receive—the overwhelming love of that embrace.

As you take in the interior of this place, you are stunned, once again, by the beauty you find. Look around and see how every detail reflects the core of you. It's amazing, isn't it?

You're invited to sit down, to relax. You sink into the most comfortable chair you have ever felt, placed in front of a large picture window with a gorgeous view of the horizon. Your heart softens with gratitude and awe. You are Home.

On a small side table to your right, you notice a notebook and pen. The cover of the notebook has your name on it, practically glowing. You pick up the notebook and feel it vibrating in your hand. This gentle but distinct buzzing jumps from the notebook into your fingertips and rapidly moves up your arms and through your body until every bit of you is buzzing with excitement, with joy, with hope, and with ideas. You are inspired to create, to put into writing the Goodness flowing through you, knowing it is not only what you need, but what the universe needs you to do.

There is nothing to limit you here—no thought, no person, no memory, and no doubt. You have been invited here for the *soul* purpose of conscious creation, which is only possible when you feel right at home, right where you belong.

Maintain this heightened level of soul awareness as you prepare to write down the inner guidance flowing through you. Consider the question posed at the top of your page; *Why Am I Here?* Allow the answers to flow onto the page as a stream of consciousness. No edits to make, no doubts to distract you. Simply write what comes automatically. You may receive words that describe emotions, or you may receive full sentences. *Who are you here, beloved?* How does it feel to be you in the comforts of Home? You have all the time you need.

Feel Goodness washing over you, All of Creation flowing through you, and joy taking hold. When you have completed your response, please move to the next page.

You will now see the following question: *What Am I Here For?*

We would ask that you allow for divine guidance to move through you, co-creating the answer with you. Before putting pen to paper, please take three deep breaths and feel us approaching. We will speak through one of the loved ones who greeted you when you arrived, with whom you feel at ease in all ways. Visualize her or him again, prepared to give voice to the truth of your Being so that you may hear it and dictate it, revealing what is written on your heart. Ask this light being who loves you so completely, *"What Am I Here For?"* Place your pen upon the paper and begin a circular motion, tracing a circle over and over until words begin to come. Simply receive them, record them—even if you're not conscious of them. You have all the time you need.

When you feel us releasing from you, and conscious thoughts disrupting the flow, the answer you need today is complete. Read what you received. Trust what you received. Honor what you received.

You may come back to this Home as often as you like, for it is part of you. But it is not meant to serve as an escape from earthly life. Rather, it exists in order to work its way into your earthly life, to ease the separation anxiety, the homesickness you experience when you are out of alignment with your soul's desires and intentions.

No parent sends his or her children away to summer camp, for example, wanting them to spend their days grief-ridden and desperate for home rather than delighting in learning new skills, bonding with fellow travelers, and gaining independence. Homesick children do not see that their misery is a choice. They accept their longing as an unchangeable state of being. That is, until they are distracted by something or someone that reminds them of joy, of contentment, of feeling cared for. They might find a friend who makes them laugh, a counselor who shows them the ropes, or an activity they love. This allows a ray of light in where there previously was none, and that is all it takes to begin expanding Goodness. Before long, these children shift from homesickness to joyful engagement, realizing what they need to make themselves at home. They move from longing to belonging.

The same such transition is required for every soul finding its way on Earth. In order to be a channel for Goodness, to consciously create and experience what you came here for, you must *choose* to turn this house into a home.

We have previously addressed ways to accomplish this; namely, to cultivate joy and break free from the chains of lack. Today, we wish to address another key component: fostering life-affirming relationships and being cognizant of their energetic impact on you.

Some refer to this life as a school, and in many ways this is accurate. With each year and phase, you have the potential to learn and grow and do so in the company of a wide variety of people.

Each of you has been assigned a family (or multiple families) of teachers. Yes, teachers. This does not mean they were or are always wise or enlightened beings but that their actions provide you with growth opportunities. And you offer the same to them.

In your pursuit of purpose, your desire to be in constant alignment with Goodness, you must sometimes experience what does *not* work in order to fully recognize and embrace what does. As you travel this purposeful path, you may see some relationships falling away. Certain people may stick to the main road while you venture off into the wild unknown. You cannot fault them for this. They are on their own journey, growing at their own pace and potentially standing in the quicksand of bitterness over your growth. Be kind, for they are hurting. Be kind, for they are moving slowly. Be kind, but do not feel beholden to them. You must keep moving.

And as you do, we urge you to use what you know to create what you need. It is imperative, on this path, that the company you keep lifts you up and sees your light. Longing for these comrades, feeling homesick for them, will not bring them to you. Rather, notice in your past relationships that which you no longer want or need, and use this information to determine what you *are* ready for. And then become it.

Make *yourself* the friend, relative, or coworker who is open-minded, big-hearted, nonjudgmental, authentic, courageous, creative, compassionate, positive, and fun-loving. If you need someone to build your confidence, build someone else's. If you need someone to talk with about spiritual growth, start speaking of it with others. If you need someone with whom you can let your guard down, encourage others to feel safe with you.

Watch as healthier, happier relationships show up in your life—perhaps they already are! Notice the shift in your energy when you are in the company of someone who sees the light in you, who wants the very best for you, and who stands arm in arm with you while marveling at the glorious horizon before you. Do you recall the bouquet of wildflowers that the bicyclist carried in her basket as we began our work together? She is delighted to share with others, and they delight in receiving them and celebrating them. Those who receive you for who you are, who honor what you have to give, and who reflect that light back are your kindred spirits.

Memorize the feeling of this vibrational match, and make it a prerequisite for the partnerships you form as you move deeper into your purpose. Expect that these spirited companions will join you in droves to support you, to celebrate you, to promote you, to hire you, and to empower you. Rather than give energy to potential naysayers who could dim your light, focus on those who will gladly hold your hand as you step into your bright future.

Do you see in these visions—collaborations of your mind and soul—how you're right where you belong, creating the *You* you were meant to be? How you're *making yourself at home?* We do. And we delight in it all. For this energetic state of well-being calls the Highest Good into being, makes use of what you've learned from discomfort, and replaces your homesickness with your holiness.

REFLECTION SEVEN

WRITE AT HOME

THE NEXT TWO PAGES OFFER SPACE FOR YOU TO RECORD WHAT
YOU RECEIVED IN THE VISUALIZATION PROVIDED BY SPIRIT. A FREE
AUDIO VERSION OF THIS GUIDED MEDITATION IS AVAILABLE ONLINE.
TO ACCESS IT, GO TO YOURINFINITEPURPOSE.COM/RESOURCES
AND INPUT THE PASSWORD MAGICMAKER.

WHO AM I HERE?

WHAT AM I HERE FOR?

INSPIRING STORIES OF INFINITE PURPOSE

FROM REACHING TO PREACHING

When Interfaith Minister and yoga teacher Lisa Sarick first began reading *Infinite Purpose*, she was feeling a little lost. Two and a half years prior, she and her family had moved to rural Pennsylvania, and though she enjoyed being a stay-at-home mom with a myriad of side projects, she felt disconnected from her purpose, unsure what she wanted to do next.

She felt pulled like a magnet to the *Infinite Purpose* teachings, and now she knows why. As soon as Spirit urged us all to give voice to our visions, clarity arrived for Lisa. She knew she was ready to step deeper into her role as a minister, joyfully leading Sunday morning services.

Lisa let her vision percolate as she continued working through Spirit's steps. She felt doubt and self-judgment lifting from her, she connected with people in her community who were eager to help, and she could feel momentum building. By the time she read the message of Step Seven, she no longer felt lost—but found. Lisa revisits this step often to be reminded that to make yourself at home is "the only way to continuously experience the serendipitous and euphoric merging of your spiritual life with your earthly life."

Just four months after Lisa completed the *Infinite Purpose* teachings, she led her first Sunday services for a new faith community she launched in Pennsylvania called SoL (Spirit of Love). Her future visions include children's programs, adult classes, and a vibrant community of members with a mission to spread love in the world.

"I am right where I am meant to be," she said. "I am noticing and acknowledging that I have everything I need, that I have unseen help and support as I create my dream, and that divine timing is at work. I'm creating the spiritual community I had dreamed of with ease and joy! I *am* Home."

To learn more about Lisa, visit lisasarick.com.

MOVING RIGHT ALONG

Several weeks after artist and writer Carissa Paige finished reading *Infinite Purpose*, she rented a U-Haul truck and removed two-thirds of the stuff in her house. Even the dining room table and chairs had to go! As she and her husband unloaded their belongings at a local thrift shop, Carissa already felt lighter.

Clearing out the clutter was powerfully symbolic for Carissa. Three months earlier, she'd found a therapist to help her work through much of the emotional clutter from her past, including growing up with an alcoholic mother. Though she'd done lots of solo work to release old patterns and beliefs, Carissa knew she needed help to clear the emotional debris that kept coming back and blocking her path. She felt herself cracking open, finally able to release her inner fears, just as the *Infinite Purpose* teachings arrived.

"I laughed out loud at the uncanniness and synchronicity of the messages," she said.

Carissa was amazed and amused by the ways each teaching aligned with her healing and creative work. In fact, a couple of days before reading Spirit's Step Two (with the parable about the man by the sea), Carissa made a mixed media painting of a girl with the infinity symbol next to her and the following words: "As if some sort of buried treasure, she arose . . . from deep within."

She was shocked by the synergies between her painting and Spirit's words and knew it was no accident. Rather, she took it as a sign that there was treasure to be found if she just kept going, kept digging, kept creating, and kept emerging. As she released fears and stories that were keeping her stuck, she felt guided to begin creating a new online course to help other women do the same. But to be fully open and ready to do that, she knew, she needed to clean house. Literally.

"There was all this stuff that no longer belonged in my life—old stories that weren't serving me, emotions I didn't know what to do with, and the stuff in my house held a lot of that energy," Carissa said. That clearing of her house helped her finally feel right at home in her own skin, in her work, and in her decision to teach again.

"I can see so clearly now that I have divine support," she said. "There's this connection to my Source—to angels and guides—who are making sure I'm not alone or even creating any of my work alone. It's part of this bigger purpose, and I feel right at home in it."

Learn more about Carissa at carissapaige.blogspot.com.

STEP EIGHT

LIGHTING THE WAY

THE DAY BEFORE LORI AND I FIRST ANNOUNCED THAT WE WERE COLlaborating with Spirit for a program called *Infinite Purpose*, unsure what we were getting ourselves into, I kept thinking back to a moment two years prior when I was sitting on the edge of Lake Superior. I could feel that my life was about to change. I even took a picture to remember the *right before*.

As you know, my intuitive abilities had been a closely guarded secret most of my life and had expanded while I healed from depression and PTSD. But the presence of spirits and angels in my midst greatly intensified after my dad's death in 2011. Though I tried my best, it was growing harder to keep everything I saw and heard under wraps.

Within hours of arriving on the rocky shores of Lake Superior to relax with a tribe of artist friends including Lori, they convinced me to do intuitive readings for each of them. One by one, each woman sat with me on or near those rocks, laughing and crying as angels, guides, and loved ones on the Other Side came through. I could see healing happening before my eyes, and something clicked for me.

Though I'd done under-the-radar readings for people before, this was the first time I really understood the power of the guidance they received and that I'd been given those abilities for a reason. For years, I'd been inspired by the words Oprah Winfrey once said were her daily prayer: "Show me how to take who I am, who I want to be, and what I can do and use it for a purpose greater than myself. Use me until you use me up."

It's what I wanted, too—for the Powers That Be to *use me up, to use my life*. But did my gifts have to be so unconventional!? I was scared of being ridiculed and rejected, of not being good enough at it, and of not knowing how to move forward.

So, I went out on the rocks alone to talk to God. "Okay, I get it," I said to the unending horizon. "You're using me. I'm grateful. I'm also scared. So, if I'm going to do this, I need instructions. Please, pretty please, show me how and when and where to use what you've given me."

I paid attention to the signs before me and the nudges within me, and it felt like the universe did everything possible to show me I was on the right path. The day I shared on my blog that I was starting to offer intuitive readings, three months' worth of sessions sold out. Every work obligation I'd hung on to, just to pay the bills, fell away and new, light-filled opportunities took their place.

And when it came time for Lori and me to reveal our collaboration with Spirit, I felt the same as I had on that rocky shore two years earlier. We had no doubt our lives were about to change. Though we didn't have the language for it yet, we were immersed in the "conscious creation" that Spirit speaks of in this next step.

As we witnessed powerful shifts among that first group of magic makers who followed the steps of *Infinite Purpose*, Lori and I were astounded by the possibilities and people (from producers to publicists to publishers) that showed up, seemingly out of nowhere, to advance our work in the world. We have frequently shared tears of joy and prayers of gratitude for the chance to experience the profound shifts and crazy-good results of walking this path. And we have no doubt that as you move into Step Eight and continue to incorporate Spirit's wisdom into your life, you'll experience the same kinds of divine interventions. We think *your* life is about to change, too.

MESSAGE FROM SPIRIT

WE ARE HERE WITH YOU NOW AS WE ALWAYS HAVE BEEN AND ALWAYS will be. Rest in the knowing you are never alone. That you felt called to these teachings, drawn in for reasons unknown, verifies your ability to hear and honor what your soul came here to do. For some, the call was loud and insistent. You could not ignore it. For others, the call was quiet. Still, you answered. Like absentmindedly humming along to the faint melody of a favorite song, you joined in, and for this we are delighted.

It is important that you know you are right where you belong and have gained from this journey precisely what you came for. You may attempt to dispute this, assuming that you should have a game plan or business plan . . . any kind of plan for moving forward.

And the truth is *you do*. Our time together and these steps we have outlined *are* your plan, beloved. It is the one you agreed to many moons ago, the one that glimmers of Goodness have revealed to you, the one that your dreams, visions, and inspirations have ignited in you. You now hold in your hands and hearts a manifesto of universal truths meant to unearth your reasons for being, free you from the chains of convention, and familiarize you with the sensation of experiencing the heightened vibrational frequency of living on *purpose*. Your individual plan for productivity and prosperity may not yet be made of paper and ink, of numbers and dates, or of certainties and strategies. We urge you to rest in the knowing that you already have everything you need to do all that you desire.

This is precisely what we have come to teach and quietly blessed your paths with as you have walked through these steps: evidence of your holiness, indications of your soul's eagerness to emerge enlightened, vast support for your awakening, and proof that your path is finding you (rather than the other way around).

As you have absorbed the truth of these teachings, you have each activated a time of accelerated growth, with no two inner journeys identical. Some have viscerally felt the internal shifts that result from a shared and rising vibration between us and you. Some have experienced changes in perception of their past and present, of pain and pleasure, which alters the trajectory and momentum of your life's work, your light-work. Some have witnessed or experienced camaraderie and compassion among kindred spirits-even perfect strangers—like never before, reducing your sense of solitude and exclusion, revealing that you *do* belong.

And some of you have already felt and seen your path appear before you, not as a complete and detailed road map, but as next steps serendipitously revealed, abundance and opportunity appearing "out of nowhere," or surprising self-revelations and invitations to heal rising to the surface. These are the combined result of fear released and joy renewed.

If such experiences seem elusive or unreachable, you know what you need to do: release fear, renew joy. You are aware of, even fooled by, what holds you back. In some cases, you allow semantics to get in your way, tripped up by a word or phrase or concept that triggers resistance, defensiveness, or a sense of lack. We have also witnessed many of you spending precious time focused on creating a name for yourself before you even know your message, your mission, or the meaning of your work. This is because your ego says you are not worthy of the magnitude of what you've come to share, that you must prove you are worthy to do anything of worth. Remember, beloved, you are made of the stars that blaze with purpose in the night sky. Of course you are enough.

Each time these fears arise, acknowledge the roadblock and then make a choice. Stand firm and let the barrier serve as justification for your continued sense of being stuck, or actively look for the detour, the scenic route that allows you to bypass the stuckness, places you on the open road, and reveals a new way to get where you're going. This is inspired action.

Welcome to a succulent life rooted in the practice of repeatedly releasing what does not serve you (and therefore, ultimately, serves no one)—a minute-to-minute, mind-and-soul practice that acts as the very foundation of your well-being. It is in this open space where you are free to fly, trusting that the sacred back roads do not lead to nowhere special, but deliver you, each day, to some place wondrous. Go forth, beloved, knowing that conscious creation can move mountains.

To live this earthly life with soulful intention, inspired action, and implicit trust is to experience the precise and stunning choreography of Goodness at work, orchestrating opportunities you could have never planned and eliminating perceived obstacles. The universe matches your vibration, energetically reflecting (and, in so doing, producing) all that is possible within your consciousness. If your energy is primarily dedicated to resisting roadblocks and defying gravity, the universe provides matched resistance. If you choose, instead, to focus your energy on surrendering to boundless grace and allowing hope to take flight, the universe matches your well-being with unlimited resources and inexplicable synchronicities. Mountains move, indeed, so that your path may be paved with golden stardust and your horizon reveals only vivid promise.

Let us retrace our steps in order to reveal your plan for moving forward in line with conscious creation. We begin in the wild unknown, your new home away from Home. The rolling hills and unmarked paths, far removed from the clogged roadways of convention, are not meant as an occasional escape, but are the place where you *belong*. You are free and clear among the wildflowers, basking in the glow of Light Eternal, not detached from the "real world," but inspired to serve it well.

As your dreams come into focus, stirring giddiness and Goodness in you, you must be the first to believe in them. Pay attention to the daydreams and night dreams that do not let you go, that come to you again in visions or visitors, nudges and signs. Speak of them out loud, and feel the power of your truth vibrating through you, lifting you up and out of stagnancy and scarcity.

Abandon all attempts to create only what you suspect will please others, and reject all notions that you are not properly equipped, educated, or connected to manifest your dreams. Let your imagination run wild. Marvel at your surroundings with childlike wonder. Explore new avenues with euphoric curiosity, and start every conversation with radical compassion. Always entertain joy. Without it, you will find yourself gasping for air, weak in the knees, and dizzied by desperation.

Rather than rushing in like wildfire to clear the obstacles that block your path, be patient, beloved. Carefully tend to your own well-being so that you have the energy—physically, mentally, and spiritually—to create or contribute where you feel moved to do so.

In Step Seven of *Infinite Purpose*, we asked you to listen closely to the whispers of your soul and to insight from the Great Beyond, writing down what came through for you. We asked you to reflect on who you are within this sacred space of letting go and living inspired. The only answers you need are those that affirm and confirm your resilience and brilliance. If your writings fall short of this intention, go deeper and listen closer. Ego has pushed aside your true essence, the part of you that sees and celebrates your divinity, but you can easily and calmly return to this question to retrieve the truth.

The second question, which asked what you are here for, instructed you to shift your attention to the wisdom of All That Is, which worked its way through you and onto your paper. Perhaps you were asked to unbridle a bold knowing. Perhaps you were told of a role you have come to fill. Perhaps you were instructed to utilize your gifts in new ways with new people. Perhaps you received news that you suspected all along but never fully honored. Perhaps you have been born into a mission that sounds so audacious, it has to be true—for you would have never tasked yourself with such a responsibility!

If you resisted the invitation, saving the question for later or denying the message received, we understand. Rejoice in the knowing that even being aware the question exists—*what are you here for?*— allows for spiritual expansion. You can always return for the resounding answers when you feel even more deeply pulled into the holiness of your true calling.

In the meantime, in service to this intention, continue developing a daily practice of releasing the psychological debris that compromises clarity. Write down the limiting beliefs that hold you back from receiving or trusting the news of your soul's desired impact on the world (see pages 159-161).

Even if the answer you received rang true from head to toe, we invite you to write down and energetically release any doubts that rise to the surface. Remember, beloved, you are *joyfully shifting into a constant state of alignment with Goodness*. Watch how abundance flows in when fear spills out onto the page, landing in its final resting place, no longer needed for false protection to validate your holding back.

Let us work together to turn these into hope and help you feel at home in the promised land of infinite purpose. We have already shown you that the All Knowing Universe sees your *true* reflection. It is now time for *you* to consciously move beyond your fear and see the same. Please look at the concerns on your paper now exposed, in the open, and shift the language from deprivation to exultation. Put into writing and feel the vibration of honoring the alternatives to, or opposites of, the limitations your ego has tried so hard to set in stone.

"I AM SCARED OF FAILING" BECOMES "I AM JOYFULLY SUCCEEDING!"

"I am scared of having no money" transforms into "I am delighted by my abundance!"

"I am scared I'm getting too old" shifts to "I am thrilled to be the perfect age!"

With these affirmations of truth taking hold, look again at why you are here, beloved. It will, undoubtedly, still feel big. So, begin small (we see no difference, after all). One step leads to many, and each one signals to the universe that you are well on your way, ready for the swirling momentum it is poised to provide.

Will some peers look cross-eyed at your enlightened way of being? Might someone mistake your inner light for insanity? Quite possibly, for many are still disconnected from their true Source of Divinity, knee-deep in rules and reservations that provide a false sense of security. It is difficult to move through such sludge, and they may thrash about in reaction to your truth telling, unsettled by the palpable difference in your energetic frequencies, fearful of what they do not understand. Know this: all is well, beloved, even if they insist it is not.

Imagine yourself in a community of people a century ago, sharing the knowledge and resources you have today. Imagine revealing your modern technology to them, such as a mobile communication device. Not only would they have never seen such a thing, but they could not comprehend its ability to connect to a world beyond. Their fear of this technology would be mighty, for what is not readily understood is often *mis*understood and brashly denounced as dangerous or irrational. Most would not be ready for such evolutionary and revolutionary innovation.

But this would be of no consequence to you as long as you remained committed to allowing your joy to be a light, attracting kindred spirits who see Goodness in you and what you share. Indeed, some people *would* see great potential in such a newfangled idea *(a new way to connect!? streaming information that defies time and space!?)*. These brave souls would rise above fear and feel moved to act upon the joyful curiosity stirring within them, asking you for more information, experimenting with innovation, and perhaps even following you into the wild unknown.

This is how new consciousness is born and expands, how souls recognize their calling—not in lightning strikes and booming voices from beyond, but by listening closely and surrendering to insatiable curiosity, to unlimited possibility, to newfangled ideas, and to universal truths that match the vibration of All That Is Good.

You are now one of those brave souls who has experienced the highs and lows of humanity and then courageously followed what stirred you awake. You feel compelled to connect in new ways to your calling, to fellow magic makers, and to the vast universe that supports you. You are receiving and leveraging these teachings, this streaming information that defies time and space. You are facing the horizon with hope and wonder, awed and validated as the obstacles shift, fear releases, and your path to purpose grows crystal clear.

You are quickly becoming proof that it is possible to cultivate deep, abiding joy—a poster child for infinite purpose. That is all it will take for others to follow and feel called to what *you* create. Do, think, make, and share whatever joyful endeavors feel like a homecoming, like a light-filled reunion with the soul of you. Let time and space fall away and doubts step aside to make room for the manifestation of your mission.

Envision yourself steeped in joy today, tomorrow, and beyond. *Feel* the emotion in it, the energy of it, and the blessed mystery surrounding it. You need not know what it is, only how you feel in the light of Unlimited Possibility. Know that in this state, you are collaborating with a universe that loves you, that delights in reflecting *your* joy, and that is immeasurably grateful for your courage to align with Goodness and create more light.

You are needed. You are beloved. You are purpose personified. Watch for magic to unfold, for mystery to swoop in, for abundance to appear, for needs to be met, and for mountains to move so that you can be the light in this world (the trailblazer, yes!) that your soul was once so excited, so eager to become. Your dreams are coming true, and therefore, so are ours. This is only the beginning. Oh joy! Oh joy! Oh joy!

REFLECTION EIGHT

STEP INTO CONSCIOUS CREATION

To aid you in this exercise, rewrite the answer you received from Spirit during Step Seven when asked *"Why are you here?"*

....

....

....

....

....

....

....

Now, write down the limiting beliefs (fears, concerns) that hold you back from trusting the news of your soul's desired impact in the world. If you didn't try the exercise, share what fears or distractions have kept you from doing so.

....

....

....

....

....

....

....

....

Per Spirit's request, craft new statements that reflect the opposite of those fears, creating powerful and true affirmations. So, "I am scared of failing" may become "I am joyfully succeeding!" Feel the vibrational shift of allowing these new statements to become truth for you.

Think of one inspired (joyful!) step you can take today to lean into Spirit's description of why you are here. Share your vision? Do some research? Offer someone your help? Write it down, and then do it! (If you can think of multiple steps, record them all!)

INSPIRING STORIES OF INFINITE PURPOSE

JOBLESS AND JOYFUL

One week before Janey Palmer dove into the teachings of *Infinite Purpose*, her long-term, full-time role as a freelance communications strategist for a major corporation ended. For the first time in eight years, there was no steady paycheck. She knew it was a sign that it was time to do something different, but the unknown still felt scary. Reading Spirit's encouraging words helped her shift from fear to faith.

"I decided to trust that all was well and that I didn't have to prove my worthiness through income," she said. "Rather, that my worthiness is a given, not something I had to earn."

For the first time in ages, Janey had plenty of time for self-reflection, time to actively and intentionally let go of the emotional baggage standing in her way: fear, jealousy, guilt, perfectionism, and negativity. When responding to challenges, Janey chose to do the opposite of what she'd always done and realized she was laughing more, smiling more, and saying "yes" to things she never would have done before. She made joy a priority, creating a new painting every week and taking improv classes.

Janey read through the final step of *Infinite Purpose* as she watched the sun rise, her husband and daughter still fast asleep, and marveled at feeling content with not knowing where her path would lead.

"I knew I could take the baby steps laid out in that message, using my feelings as my guide," Janey said. "I felt so very blessed and happy in that moment."

For the next three months, she focused on trusting that the right things would show up for her at the perfect time rather than panicking about not having a job. Whenever doubt crept in, she turned to Spirit's words and also tapped into her own intuition.

Eventually, a job opportunity practically fell into her lap. She felt nervous getting ready for the interview, but when she opened her car door, there was a feather sitting on the driver's seat! Janey *knew* it was a sign that she was heading into that interview with divine support. She felt right at home with the three women she met that day, and she was offered a long-term contract to do challenging, fascinating work.

A FEATHER IN HER CAP

A lifelong creative spirit, Lisa Tsering came to *Infinite Purpose* in the midst of an identity crisis. In her soul, she always knew she was an artist, but fear held her back. What if she wasn't talented or successful enough to be a "real" artist? So, she devoted most of her energy to being a mom, a wife, and a graphic designer, dabbling in art projects on the side.

In a moment of bravery, Lisa submitted some of her work to Alena Hennessy, an artist and teacher she greatly admired, to be considered for inclusion in her upcoming painting book. Lisa decided that if her art was chosen from the sea of applicants, she'd consider it a sign that it was time to begin calling herself and living as an artist.

As Lisa began reading *Infinite Purpose* and Spirit asked that she name three trailblazers who inspired her, she was quick to name Alena as one of them. Within days, she received news that two of her paintings—both of feathers—were chosen to be included in Alena's book!

Lisa was incredibly happy and totally terrified. She started to have conversations with Spirit in her head, revealing how scared she was, unsure how to truly become an artist. And that's when she first heard a gentle whisper that said, "Follow the feathers." She heard that phrase repeatedly as she moved through the teachings, but she wasn't sure what it meant. So she waited, trusting more would come.

Just after finishing the last message, Lisa felt a clear knowing and began to see a path appear before her: she would create a new feather-inspired piece of artwork each day for a year. She called the project *365 Feathers: A Creative Journey* and posted each creation on social media. Within a couple of months, she'd been a featured artist in several online publications and was gaining a following. This fueled her decision to commit to her art full time.

"People that I'd never expected to be impacted by my art are reaching out to me, saying that I inspire them, and I am in awe of it," Lisa said. "I am showing up for the art that is wanting to come through me and guiding me. I have moments where I'm just overcome by gratitude for the beauty that has taken place since I found *Infinite Purpose*."

You can follow Lisa's journey as an artist at instagram.com/LisaMarieTsering.

ONLY THE BEGINNING

AS WE WERE BUSILY WORKING TO BRING THIS BOOK TO LIFE, WE CONsidered writing a "conclusion" chapter. But that didn't feel quite right. Not only is there no end to *infinite* purpose, but Spirit actually acknowledged in Step Eight that this is only the beginning. So that is what we'll call these last pages. Not a conclusion, but a brave and bold beginning.

If you've worked your way through Spirit's wise teachings, absorbed the stories and artwork meant to bring those teachings to life, and taken time to deeply reflect on the questions asked of you and actions suggested to you, then you understand what we mean, and what Spirit means. You can probably feel the beginning of something new, something brave, and something beautiful churning within you. Or maybe you've already set the wheels in motion and you're beginning to see good things rushing in. Don't stop there. Keep going.

Look closely and you'll notice something about most of the sixteen brave hearts who graciously allowed us to share *their* stories of infinite purpose. They didn't just experience profound shifts *while* they read Spirit's teachings, but in the weeks and months *after*. As they intentionally kept applying Spirit's instructions to their own circumstances, often revisiting the words that held deep meaning for them, their momentum continued to build. Resources arrived. Joy emerged. Confidence crystallized. Kindred spirits appeared. Opportunities grew.

The birth of this book has been awesome to witness and incredible to experience. Yes, we, too, keep coming back to Spirit's teachings, not just because we've turned them into a book, but because the more we apply their wisdom to our work—both individually and together—the more we're awed by what transpires. We still face challenges, of course, but they seem so much easier to work through with Spirit's guidance. And when fear creeps in, we know just what to do. We will continue to leverage these steps, frequently opening the pages to find the wisdom that we need, and we invite you to do the same.

We believe having a tribe of people who support and celebrate you, and vice versa, is vitally important as you dive into this process and emerge from the teachings ready to light up the world (or at least your corner of it). We love hearing that book clubs and study groups are forming around this work— so cool! Be sure, too, to join the *Infinite Purpose* community at Facebook.com/InfinitePurpose. You'll find inspiring updates and a circle of fellow magic makers who are absorbing and implementing these teachings.

As we've said from the start, this book was carefully, lovingly, and purposefully made for *you*. Yes, we handled the logistics of bringing it to life, but Spirit led us in every step of the journey and, we believe, has intentionally called you here to gently guide every step of yours. Our greatest hope is that you now see and feel you are a gifted magic maker with earthly and celestial support at your fingertips.

We're sending you so much love as you step into the bright light of your infinite purpose.

USE THESE BLANK PAGES IN ANY WAY YOU CHOOSE: WRITE DOWN ADDITIONAL REFLECTIONS, CAPTURE NEW IDEAS, OR MAKE NOTES ABOUT INSIGHTS THAT HAVE TOUCHED YOU. NEED MORE BLANK SHEETS OR REFLECTION WORKSHEETS? DOWNLOAD THEM AT YOURINFINITEPURPOSE.COM/RESOURCES USING THE PASSWORD MAGICMAKERS.

LIV LANE

SPIRIT LIFTER. LIFE SHIFTER.

LIV LANE IS AN INTUITIVE ADVISER WHO HAS INSPIRED THOUSANDS OF brave-hearted, open-minded women to leap into their bright futures with clarity and confidence.

For nearly two decades, Liv built a successful career in communications as a radio host, publicist, and media company co-founder, quietly leveraging her life-long intuitive gifts to guide her decisions. But, feeling called to a deeper mission creatively and spiritually, she left corporate America in 2007. Today, Liv teaches popular personal-growth classes and workshops, conducts individual intuitive readings, and speaks about the power of purpose, passion, and inspired action to audiences across the U.S.

Liv lives in the Twin Cities with her husband Brad, their two sons, and an invisible army of angels. Find her online at livlane.com.

LORI PORTKA

HAPPINESS THROUGH ART

LORI PORTKA IS A LICENSED ARTIST WHOSE MISSION IS TO SPREAD LOVE and happiness through the art she creates. Lori's distinctive paintings feature vibrant imagery and life-affirming messages dedicated to kindness, gratitude, and being true to yourself.

In 2015, Lori's 100 Thank Yous project was the subject of a widely-celebrated short documentary film called *Gratitude Grows*. Her colorful artwork appears on greeting cards, prayer flags, and stationary merchandise at hundreds of retailers around the world.

Lori lives in Asheville, N.C. with her husband Jay and their gentle-hearted greyhounds. To learn more about Lori and her work, visit loriportka.com.

For *Infinite Purpose* updates,
merchandise and exclusive content,
visit **yourinfinitepurpose.com**.